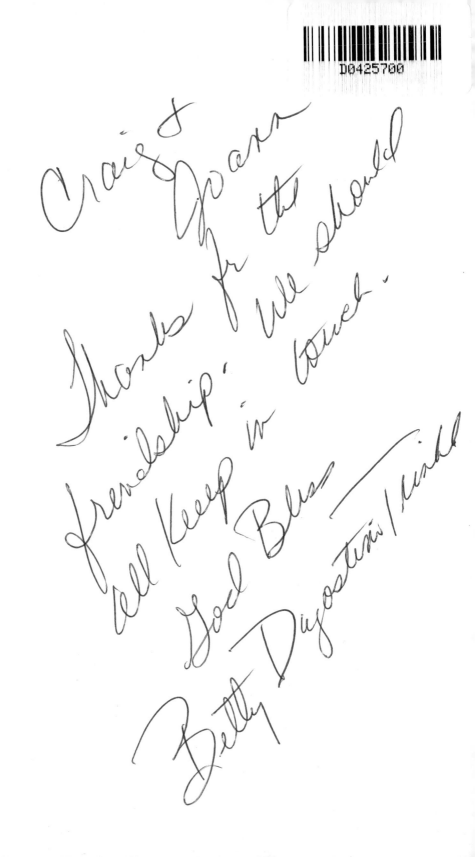

Craig & Joann

Thanks for the friendship. We should all keep in touch.

God Bless

Betty Dagostino/Tisdale

Tim McGraw

A Mother's Story

Tim McGraw

A Mother's Story

by Betty "McMom" Trimble

D'Agostino/Dahlhauser/Ditmore Publishing

© 1996 D'Agostino/Dahlhauser/Ditmore Publishing
All rights reserved.

Editor: Currey Copple

Design, typography, and text production:
TypeByte Graphix

ISBN: 1-886371-32-6

D'Agostino/Dahlhauser/Ditmore Publishing
P.O. Box 128138
Nashville, Tennessee 37212
(800) 776-3650

Assistants
Diana Henderson—Simply Read Literary Consulting/Manager-Agent
Eric Dahlhauser—Total Management/Business Manager-Publisher
Ree Ditmore—Total Management/Consultant-Publisher
Richard Courtney—Eggman Publishing/Consultant
Beth Seigenthaler—Thomas P. Seigenthaler/Publicity
Rea Anne Rubenstein/McMom Photo
Daniela Federrici/Tim McGraw Photo
Donna Paz—Paz & Associates/Consultant
George Schnitzer—Schnitzer Communication/Consultant
Lisa Hughes/Consultant
Mary Reeves/Consultant
Sue Rice/Typist
Cover Design by: Wesley Ligon—Mad Dog Designs

This book is dedicated to my children:
Tim, Tracey, and Sandy.

I love you guys with all of my heart.
I'm very proud to say I'm your mom.

To my husband:

> *My knight in shining armor!*
> *I love you always!*

A special thanks to Mary Reeves:

For being my best friend for some 32 years and for her help in putting this book together.
> *I love ya girl!*

Acknowledgements

I want to say thank you to my manager/agent, Diana Henderson. Thanks for all your hard work and support. You're great!

Eric Dahlhauser, thanks for believing in my project. Here's to more projects together.

To my wonderful husband for all his support with this project. I know you've been neglected this last year while I was working on the book, and I want you to know I appreciate all your help and understanding. I love you very much.

To all my friends and family, *THANK YOU!!!*

Preface

I was named Elizabeth Ann Dagostino, but everyone has always called me Betty. I was born March 10, 1948, in Washington, D.C. My father, John Dagostino, passed away over five years ago. His parents came to the United States from Italy. My grandmother was expecting my dad when they immigrated to this country. My dad was a television repairman and had an appliance store, like a McDuff store, before there were McDuff stores. He met my mom, Annie Catherine Welch, when he was in the Army, in a little town called Bunkie, Louisiana. He moved the barefoot country girl to the big city.

My mom and her family lived in Louisiana. They were mostly farmers. We would go visit my grandparents' farm every other Thanksgiving. That's about the only time we saw them, and it was different from our life in the city. My brother, Johnny (we called him Johnny Boy), who now lives in Arkansas, and my sister, Regina, who lives in Texas, and I loved feeding the chickens and seeing cows, horses, and cotton fields—things we never saw in D.C. My brother is eleven months younger than me and my sister is seven years younger. My dad worked all the time. We usually didn't see much of him until Sunday. My mom was a housewife.

When I was seven, we moved to Jacksonville, Florida. We had vacationed a lot in Florida, so we moved there, and Dad opened his business. We were a middle-class family living in a nice two-story home with a swimming pool. We had a good life. My mom was strict. She wasn't the kind of mom who played with you. She was the MOM!

We grew up Catholic because my dad was Catholic. My mom came from a long line of Southern Baptists. I made my first Holy Communion and my Confirmation. I took piano and dance lessons. I loved dancing. I loved singing, too. I was one of these kids who sang all the time. In the car, I drove everyone crazy. My dad played the violin. I loved all kinds of music: jazz, country, rock, Dixie. And I loved musicals, especially "My Fair Lady." I just loved music.

As I grew up, I learned every kind of dance I could. As a teenager in Florida, we had teenage clubs, where they'd play records, dance, and sometimes have live bands. "American Bandstand" was my regular Saturday show. Then came "Where the Action Is!" and "Hullabaloo."

I entered a lot of dance contests and always won. It got to the point that I had to be a judge, because they wouldn't let me win anymore. When I was old enough to drive, my girlfriend and I would visit the local radio stations. I got a job answering the request line at one. I talked to the manager/program director about putting dancers on stage when they did promotions and big shows. He liked the idea and the radio station held auditions. We hired five dancers. I was the leader. My girlfriend Mary Jay Bryant, who had been my friend since seventh grade, and I worked up all the choreography. We performed at openings of supermarkets and at shows where we met stars like the Dave Clark Five, Freddie and the Dreamers, Dino, Desi and Billy, Billy Joe Royal, the Beach Boys, the Shangra-las, and Dusty Springfield. It was great!

My mom and dad started having problems when I was 16. Mom was going to beauty school and she and Dad ar-

Betty in high school

Betty's dancing days

gued a lot. Things were just not as happy as they were. When I was 17, they started separating off and on. In 1966, about a month before my 18th birthday, they finally divorced. Mom, Regina, and I moved into a two-bedroom apartment. My mom worked as a hairdresser and was single, so she was gone a lot. I had a steady boyfriend for almost a year. He was a senior and I was a junior. We went to the Prom in May, and a month later we broke up. It seemed like the worst year of my life. Little did I know . . .

Betty's parents in 1948 prior to her birth

Betty loved playing cowboys

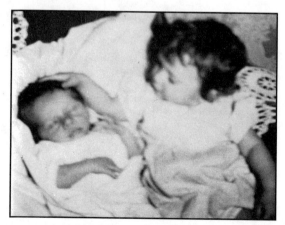

Johnny Boy and Betty in 1949

Home in D.C. that
Betty's dad built

Betty and
Johnny Boy

Betty

Betty's first Communion

Johnny Boy and Betty
in their backyard

Betty first grade

Their home before their parents' divorce

Betty and Johnny Boy
playing cowboys

Betty, Johnny Boy and Regina

Johnny Boy, Regina and
Betty

Betty's mom, Betty and Betty's stepdad

Betty, her dad and Regina

Foreword

You know the old saying, "What goes around comes around." I think in most cases that's true. Things in my life have come full circle and I believe that God looks out for us all. You live your life the best way you can, treat people the way you would want to be treated, and you'll be all right. God has always helped me. I've had some bad times, and I've had some great times. But I've always had Him to talk to and . . . He does talk back.

I'm a bookkeeper/office manager. In 1978 I was working at the Triffin Inn Restaurant and Rusty Nail Lounge in West Monroe, Louisiana. I always knew when school was out for the day, because my phone would start ringing. One of my kids—Tim, 11; Tracey, 10; or Sandy, 8—would be on the other end, saying, "Mom, she did this," or "he won't leave me alone." Just another typical day for a working mom, until the day I got the call that I had been dreading for a long time. A bad time in my past had finally come up, and I had to deal with it. It was Tim, my oldest. I could tell instantly that something was seriously wrong. He begged me to come home. My heart was racing with the fear only a mother can understand: when her child needs her and she's at work.

"What's wrong? Is anyone hurt?" I asked, not fully understanding what was happening.

"No, and no one's bleeding either. I just need to talk to you. It's important, Mom." I knew it was something I needed to take care of right away, by the tone in Tim's voice. And I knew it was very important, if even just to him. So I left work early. I locked my office and told Shirly, the restaurant manager, that I had to go home for an emergency. I got home around 4:00 p.m. The girls were outside playing ball with their babysitter, Cathy. I called for Tim, and as I went through the front door I saw him lying on his bed.

"What's wrong?" I asked. His face was white as he sat up and handed me a piece of paper. It was a document that I had buried from my mind, dreading ever having to face the story that the words on the piece of paper told all too well.

"What's this?" Tim asked.

"Where did you get this?" I replied. I could not believe that the secret I had held so long was suddenly in the hands of my son. Oh, God, why now? I wasn't ready for this.

"I found it in the metal box in your closet. I had to have an old picture for school. We're writing about things we liked to do when we were little and I was going to write about riding horses with Dad and needed a picture. But he ain't my dad, is he?"

Tim had found his birth certificate! I was shocked. I didn't think I'd have to deal with this for several more years. He was only 11, and I was planning on telling him when he was 16, when he could understand better. I looked back at my baby. He was so upset. I slowly sat on the bed beside him, hugged him, and said. "Tim, I'm so sorry you found out this way."

"It's not true, is it?" he asked. "Horace is my dad, right?"

All my hidden fears were now reflected in his young eyes. That night more than 11 years ago had changed my life forever. Now it was about to change the life of my precious son.

"No, Tim. I was planning on telling you when you were older. Horace is not your dad. Tug McGraw is your father." Tim and I were both crying. I walked outside and asked Cathy to take the girls out for a while. Tim and I needed time alone to work all of this through. I gave Cathy some money for burgers, and she left with the girls. I went back inside to Tim. He just kept looking at his birth certificate.

I could only guess what was going through his young mind. He was, even at his young age, very athletic and was a huge baseball fan. It always seemed ironic to me that Tim had several baseball cards of his favorite players displayed on his wall, and Tug McGraw was one of them. I can still remember the first time I noticed it. It almost floored me. I wondered what he would think when the day came for me to tell him.

Tim said, "Tug McGraw, the famous baseball player, the baseball cards on my wall, is my dad! Are you sure, Mom?"

"Yes, honey, I'm sure."

"Does he know where I am and have I ever seen him?"

Memories poured into my mind as though I was right back in Jacksonville, Florida, at age 18, hoping that all of this wasn't really happening. How do you explain to a child who has known only love that decisions were made that I had no control over. It had seemed that I was doing all I could do, and it felt right at the time, but it could be difficult for a young boy to understand.

"No you haven't ever seen him; nor has he ever seen you. He knows about you, but he chose his career instead of us, and I chose you. I love you, Tim! Do you hate me for not telling you?"

"No, Mom. I love you. I could never hate you."

"Tim, I swear to you I was going to tell you." Tim and I both had tears streaming down our faces. I knew we needed to get out of the house. Being outside had always helped me clear my head, especially when I could walk on the beach. There were no beaches in this small Louisiana town, so a ride in the car would have to do. "Let's go wash our faces and then we'll go for a ride and I'll try to explain things to you as best as I can."

"Mom, will I ever get to meet my real dad?"

"I don't know sweetie. I just don't know." I walked to the bathroom, the tears flooding my eyes now. I had put all of this way in the back of my mind, and now all the memories of what had happened and the emotions were swelling up all over again.

Chapter 1

I can still remember that sunny day in June 1966. I was with my friends, Mary, Joyce, Clara, Marilyn, and Sandy and my little sister, Regina. My sister, mother, and I lived in a second-floor apartment. We girls were all lying out sunning on the grass outside our apartment. We'd walk over to the pool to swim and lie in the sun. Some boys began tossing a football around. They'd miss it and it would land over by us. They'd come get it, smile and say hi. Naturally, we girls would all giggle, blush, and pretend to ignore them. Finally, after a while Joyce said, "The next time one comes over, ask him his name, Betty."

Mary said, "I dare you!" She knew I'd do it then. I don't think there is a better time in a girl's life than when she's with her friends and everyone is carefree and having a good time. Life is so simple: you meet people, flirt, and never think anything of it.

They were good-looking guys. It was just a few seconds before one of them came back. He had brown hair and was real cute. So on Mary's dare, I got up, slowly strolled over to where they were, and asked him his name.

"Tug," he said.

"What?" I said.

"T-U-G, Tug," he replied.

I said, "Strange name."

"What's yours?" he asked.

"Betty," I answered.

"Hi, Betty." He then ran off chasing the football. I didn't think much more about him, just that I hadn't backed down on Mary's dare.

We stayed about ten more minutes and then went upstairs. Everyone had to leave except Mary, who was staying over. Mary and I had been friends since seventh grade. She was always spending the night, because she had all brothers at home. We always did things together and talked about everything including our innermost secrets. She lived on the other side of town, and even though we both had other friends, we were best friends.

After we had taken our showers, we got dressed and began fixing something to eat. All of a sudden, we heard a loud banging. It sounded like it was coming from the floor. I went to the door. Nothing. I went out on the balcony. There was this "Tug" person holding a broom. He had been beating on his ceiling, which was my floor.

"Hey, Betty, you got any bleach?" He must have watched to see where our apartment was. I said I'd check. By the time I found it, he was at the door holding a cup. "I've got to wash my baseball uniform," he said.

"Aren't you a little big to still be playing baseball?" I laughed.

"I'm a pro baseball player with the Jacksonville Suns," he replied.

"Oh, that's really cool," I said. I could tell he wanted me to be impressed with that. He was just a cute guy to me though; I was not into sports. I gave him the bleach.

He said thanks, and then said, "Have you ever been to a game?"

"My dad took us once when I was younger."

"You guys want to go tonight?" he asked. I said sure.

Seemed like a great trade to me, bleach for baseball tickets. He said he'd leave the tickets at the gate.

I called Mom at work and asked her if we could use the car to go to the game. She said yes, if we took my sister, because she was going out with friends. I said okay. So we ate, changed clothes, and headed to the ball park. There were four tickets under the name "Betty" at the ball park, but only Mary, Regina, and I went. They were great seats right behind the dugout. We picked up a program and while thumbing though it, we saw a picture of Tug. According to the bio, his full name was Frank Edwin McGraw, but people called him by his nickname. He was the pitcher and we found out that he was 22. We were having a super time. Once Tug looked up and waved at us. We thought that was neat.

When the game was over, we went to our usual dining place, the Krystal. We talked about how cool we looked waving at the ball players like we really knew them. Then we went home and went to bed.

The next day I got up and got ready for summer school. I had just finished my junior year and had failed English, so I had to go to summer school or take two English classes the next year. Needless to say, I chose summer school. Mom took my sister to work with her and dropped me off at school. Summer school was so boring. I wanted to be at the beach, not in a hot classroom. At noon, Mom picked me up. She said we could take her back to work and keep the car to go to the beach. So we swung by and got Mary, and to the beach we went. While we were at the beach, it started raining and we headed home. I took Mary to her house, and Regina and I went home. Tug was standing outside as we came up the walk.

"How'd you like the game?" he yelled.

"It was fun," I said. "But you left four tickets and we only used three."

"Well, I thought you and Mary would bring your boyfriends with you."

"We aren't seeing anyone right now," I replied. "My boyfriend and I broke up a couple of months ago."

"Sorry, but hey, that's good," he said. He then told me that he and his roommates were having a party and asked if my girlfriends and I would like to come.

"I'll check," I said. "Thanks." Then he yelled at me to be sure all the girls were over 18.

That sounded very odd to me, but I said okay. I couldn't wait to call Mary, but she couldn't go. She had to do something with her brother. So I called my friend Marilyn. She said sure. We decided she'd stay the night with me. I called Mom. She said we could go but not until she got home. So I did my chores, fixed dinner, took a bath, and started to pick out my clothes. I just had to look special. This was a cute guy.

Trying to decide what to wear I got a little mad, I was so tiny most of my clothes made me look like I was 12. When Marilyn got there we finally decided on my outfit: blue shorts, white sandals, and a white ruffled top. I took extra care with my make-up and hair, since of course that's a girl's art. It had to be just right. I said, "Marilyn, how do I look?"

She said, "Great, Betty! You look 18!"

"I am 18!" I said. I didn't look my age so she thought I'd like that remark. All my friends looked older than me. Mom was always telling me I'd be glad later when I got older. (You know she was right. I love it. But don't tell her.) We got ready and waited on Mom.

It took Mom forever to get home. We kept watching out-

The apartment where Betty's mom, sister and she lived

Betty's high school

side while people were arriving to make sure we were dressed all right. So far, everyone was wearing shorts, so we'd fit in okay. Mom finally got home at 8 p.m. I told her I couldn't believe it took her so long. We'd been ready for two hours. She said we didn't need to seem so anxious and we had to have a talk (more like a lecture) before we went.

"Now," Mom said. "If these people are drinking, you two do not drink anything."

"Mom, I don't drink and never have," I said.

"Well," she said, "Don't start. Just don't drink anything unless you fix it yourself. You want to make sure no one puts anything in your Coke."

My mom always worried about stuff like that. "Be home by 11," she said. "If this party starts getting wild, come home early. And be good!"

"We promise. Can we please go?" I said.

"I don't like this: you going to his apartment," Mom said.

"Mom, he has three roommates. There'll be a lot of people there. Don't worry."

"If people start leaving, you girls come home."

"Mom, we will. I promise. I'm not a baby."

I checked the mirror one last time, and then we headed downstairs. I told Marilyn I was nervous. I said, "Watch. We'll get there and they'll treat us like babies." I was older than Marilyn, but she looked older. She was 5'6" and about 145 pounds. I was 5'1" and 96 pounds. My size always made me feel too young, a fate worst then death when you're 18.

We headed downstairs to Tug's apartment, where the party was, and knocked on the door. The door opened and some guy was standing there. He said, "Tugger, your little girlfriends are here." Tug told him to knock it off and told us to come in. I gave the guy who opened the door a drop-dead look. We were introduced to the other guys and girls. Almost all the guys were ball players. Tug showed us some trophies he had and some pictures. We just talked and sat around listening. The guys were talking baseball. One of the girls was very nice; another one was kind of snooty and wanted to know how old I was. She just snickered. That made me feel like such a baby. They were drinking beer. Marilyn and I had a Coke, which I opened myself!

About 10 p.m., people were leaving, so I said I guess we needed to go. Tug offered to walk us home. I thought that was real nice of him. When we got to the door, Marilyn went in and left us there to talk alone. I told him that it was a nice party and thanked him again. He gave me a sweet good-night kiss and said maybe we could go to the movies one night when the team was off. I said that would be great.

I could not wait to get in and talk to Marilyn. I had to tell her he kissed me and, of course, call my friend Mary and tell her. We talked over an hour, then I went to bed. The next Monday morning was the last day of summer school. I noticed that Tug and the guys hadn't been around for a couple of days. I guessed the team was on the road.

Chapter 2

I had worked part time at the radio station off and on answering the request line. I didn't have regular hours, and with my parents' divorce, and summer school, I couldn't go very often. I mentioned earlier on that I had put together a dance group. Dancing was my favorite thing. I liked singing too, but I knew I could really dance. Since Mom and Dad's divorce everything had changed so much. We had only one car, so it was harder to go to the small shows and dance every weekend. The apartment was small so there wasn't a lot of room for practice.

Rehearsals were harder, because we couldn't afford to rent a professional studio. In his TV repair shop, my father had used mirrors that were about two feet by three feet to see the front of TV screens as he repaired them. When I saw the mirrors, I knew how to solve the rehearsal problem. I had just enough mirrors to line up against the wall on the floor in a large walk-in closet in our apartment, we could see our feet as we worked on our routines.

The dance group was my idea. I was the lead dancer and did the choreography with Mary. She was the second dancer. Three other girls danced with us when we needed a full dance team. I came up with the idea of the dance team from shows like "Where the Action Is." The Action Dancers danced with all the acts on that show. So I got the idea to go to Buddy Moore, the station manager at WAPE

Radio in Jacksonville, Florida, and suggest we dance for the station. He liked the idea. So in the summer of 1964, at age 16, I guess you could say I had started a career, and it was fun. We would do little things around town such as teen dances, radio station remotes, and grand openings.

And then our big break came. I got a call from the station manager, Buddy. The radio station was putting on a big concert, the "Dick Clark Caravan" with Paul Revere and the Raiders, B.J. Thomas, Lou Christie, Dino, Desi and Billy, Tommy Roe, and the Action Dancers. I was so excited when the radio station called. We were going to be dancing with the Action Dancers. "Where the Action Is" was one of my favorite shows, and I wanted to be a dancer just like the Action Dancers! I called Mary. We had to work on our choreography and get our costumes fixed up. Marilyn made all our costumes, so we had to see if any buttons were missing or hems hanging. We cleaned our white boots so we'd look sharp! The show was on Friday only one week away. This was our first big Coliseum show. We had done smaller ones at the Civic Center and two other smaller shows at the Coliseum, but this was a big one!

Normally, we would dance with the opening acts at Coliseum concerts. (The larger shows were booked there because the seating capacity was over 11,000.)

The exception was with Freddie and the Dreamers. Freddie wanted us to do the "Freddie" (a dance he made up) with him. (At the Civic Center, where the seating was 4,000, we danced with all the acts, with no union restrictions.)

Mom said we could use the car that night. My sister would stay with my aunt and uncle. Mom was hardly ever home, so it was a lot easier to get to do things. She'd still tell me to be home by 11, but she was never there at 11 to know when I got home. We pulled up to the Coliseum back

Freddy of Freddy & the Dreamers

Dave of The Dave Clark Five

Chad and Jeremy

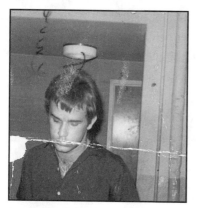

Lou Cristy

A member of the McCoys

door and got out. We were always early. Anxious, I guess. We always had the backstage bathroom for a dressing room. The "stars" got the real dressing rooms. Mary had made a star for the bathroom door as a joke. Then we practiced our routines. We were dressed and ready when the buses rolled in with the Action Dancers. Everything was great. We were going on in 20 minutes. Then, everything went crazy! The Action Dancers said if we couldn't produce union cards, we couldn't go on, not even with the opening act. If we went on, they would refuse to perform. We had never had this problem before. I guess it was because there were other dancers on the show, and we were local.

All the girls in our act were mad. I calmed them down and explained we'd have to step aside. People paid to see the Action Dancers, not us. They didn't like it (I didn't like it), but we all agreed. A few of the performers were upset by the stance the Action Dancers had taken. We had already performed with some of the acts in prior shows. Although this was our first time meeting Lou Christie, he told us he wanted us to dance with him on stage, and, quite frankly, he didn't care what the Action Dancers wanted. I thanked him but respectfully declined, not wanting to get in the middle of a union dispute.

Mark Lindsey, the lead singer of Paul Revere and the Raiders, came over to talk to us. We were clowning around and acting like we had no idea who he was. Of course, we knew who he was immediately, as they were an extremely popular group, but we wanted to give him a hard time anyway. *I was to see Mark Lindsey again years later, as you will see, and I reminded him of this incident.*

We always got along great with the acts. It was fun. We got to do what a lot of kids dream of—meeting their favorite star. The stars were always very nice. The episode with the Action dancers was the only time we ever had a problem. We were always backstage talking and getting ideas from everybody. We had met some great stars at shows we didn't dance at. Not all shows were right for our performances, like the Beach Boys, for example. They were the most popular group around other than The Beatles and Elvis. When we did dance for big shows like that, it was only for the opening acts. But we did get to meet the Beach Boys and talk to them. They are terrific guys.

I guess some of the acts we had performed with prior to that night had mentioned our abilities to the tour manager of the Action Dancers. He said he had heard we were good dancers and asked if we would like an audition with the TV show "Where The Action Is." I was ecstatic! Everything I wanted was starting to fall into place. I couldn't believe it. He left me two forms to mail to him, one for me and one for Mary. Mary was only 17 at the time and had to wait until she was 18 to officially audition. Since I was already 18, I completed my form and gave it back to him. I had always loved dancing! I wanted to be Shirley MacLaine. I also sang occasionally with local bands; I could sing, but I was no Barbra Streisand. But I knew I was a good dancer. So look out, Broadway!

We gathered our things together and went home after the show. We were excited, but a little down too, because we didn't get to dance. When we got home, I noticed a light on downstairs. I guess Tug and the guys are back, I thought.

Mary and I got up early. Mom wasn't home and Regina was still at my uncle's, so we left a note and headed for the beach. We had heard there was a "go-go" dance contest on the beach with a fifty dollar first prize and decided that we would enter, just Mary and me. We wanted new costumes and needed money for material.

Most of the girls who entered were wearing bikinis; they worked at different topless night clubs in town. We had on white dresses Marilyn had made with white tassels all over. Well, we won! After it was over, I dropped Mary off first, then went on to my apartment. As I was walking up the sidewalk, Tug yelled out for me to come swimming with him. I told him maybe later I would.

Chapter 3

The door was unlocked when I put the key into it. Daddy was there sitting on the couch. This bothered me as my dad and I hadn't been getting along very well since the divorce and I was not used to him visiting our apartment. He had wanted me to live with him because he thought mom would change her mind and reconcile with him if I did. I had refused.

My brother went to live with my dad. He was mad at my mom, blaming her for the divorce. He didn't understand. I felt my mom and my sister needed me. If Mom wasn't happy, that was her business. I didn't want them to divorce, but it wasn't my decision. My mom and I had talked some. She said she was unhappy and didn't know if she still loved my dad or not (she had married very young). I told her I was almost grown and would be going to college and hopefully pursuing my dancing career, so she didn't need to worry about me. Johnny was just a year younger than me. Regina was the one she should worry about when making her decision. That's the only time we really talked about it. Whether I agreed or not, it was her decision.

Johnny Boy just didn't understand. I don't know if she talked to him or not, but they were distant from each other for a long time. It took them a while to reconcile and for Johnny to understand; now they are very close. I missed Johnny when he wasn't living with us. He handled things his way.

Regina was there with Dad when I walked into the apartment. I guess Dad had picked up her up from my uncle's. I asked, "What are you doing here?"

"You and Regina are going to stay with me until your mother gets back," Dad said.

"Gets back? Where did she go?"

"She went to Miami with her boyfriend, and she said when she returns she'll decide whether we get back together or not. If we do, we'll move to Louisiana."

I threw a fit! I didn't even know Mom had a boyfriend. I was not going to go with him. We argued and he finally left, taking the car keys so I couldn't drive Mom's car until she got back. But I stood my ground. I called Mary, but she was gone. I wanted Mary to come get me.

I sat around and cried for a while. Then I took a shower and headed to the pool. Tug and a few people were still there. He could tell I'd been crying, so he asked what was wrong. I told him the whole story. We talked a long time. He told me about his parents' divorce. He and his two brothers grew up living with his dad. We stayed by the pool for a long time talking, then I told him I needed to try to call Mary again. Tug told me I could call her from his apartment. Since his was closer, we went there for me to use the phone. Mary still wasn't home. Tug fixed us a Coke and we sat on the couch and talked some more. No one was home; we were all alone.

He reached over and kissed me. He was so sweet. He said, "You know, everything always works out for the best." Well, quickly things got out of hand, and I ended up having my first sexual experience. Even worse, with a guy I hardly knew who was older than I. I always thought my first time would be on my wedding night with someone I had known and dated for years. I was so scared and embarrassed. I just knew he must have been thinking I was such a baby and knew nothing at all about sex. Kissing was all I had ever done. I got out of his apartment as fast as I could, feeling totally stupid and confused. I ran upstairs, took a shower, and cried. How could this happen? How could I have let this happen? Oh, God, please help me. I'm not that kind of girl.

Tug came to the door a couple of times that night, but I ignored him. I called Mary, and she and her brother came over to get me. I was so ashamed of myself. I had dated one boy for over a year and we had never done anything. We both said that we wanted to wait for marriage. And now this, with someone I hardly knew. I couldn't believe this had happened to me.

Mary could tell something was wrong, but I didn't say anything because her brother was in the car. When we got to her house, Mary and I went to her room. I started crying and told her what had happened. She started crying and said, "Don't worry. You're not the first girl in the world to have sex with a guy that way. Try not to be so upset. Everything will be fine. You'll forget all about it soon." I looked at her, she looked at me, and we hugged. Mary was the only person I could confide in. I went home the next day to get some clothes. There was a note from Tug, on the door. "Call me," it said. I threw it away.

I stayed at Mary's until Monday. We stayed out on the beach until late in the evening. We didn't talk; just walked. The beach was my solace. I had done the same thing when my parents divorced. Just walking, and listening to the ocean always made things go away for a while. (I missed that after I left Florida.) When I got home, Mom was there. I asked her what was going on, and she said she didn't want to talk now. She said we would talk later. Mom never liked to talk about anything. She said Tug had called a couple of times. I said fine and went to my room.

I stayed in my room all day. Mom and Regina were leaving for a while and asked if I wanted to go. I told them I wasn't feeling well and would stay home. I wasn't feeling well, all right. I felt sick, sick inside! I guess I was disappointed in myself for letting things get out of hand. I had more sense than that, I thought. I kept going over in my head what had happened and what I had done wrong. How had I let this happen?

August was hot and this summer was not fun like summers past. I guess it was the problems with my family. We had always lived in a nice house with a pool and I had been able to have friends over and give parties. It wasn't the same now. With all that was happening in my life, I was outgrowing things or growing up, I guess. There were a number of concerts coming to town that the radio stations wanted Mary and me to perform for, but I couldn't get excited about it. As important as my dancing was to me, it just didn't matter anymore.

I finally got Mom to talk about her and Daddy. She told me that she didn't have a boyfriend, and she had gone to Miami with friends to get away from Daddy for a while. I begged her not to go away like that again. Coming home and finding Daddy there was so upsetting, particularly not knowing what was going on. She apologized and said that it would not happen again.

Time passed and a few times when Mary and I, or Regina and I, would be walking home, Tug would yell from his sliding back door to me. I would just keep walking. I had not talked to him since that night, nor did I want to. It was now the end of August and almost time for school to start.

Mom came home one night and said we were moving. She said she just couldn't afford the apartment, and Daddy wouldn't help. She said Daddy had left the state and moved to Louisiana with Johnny Boy. Mom had found a small house at the beach. Until we got settled, Regina was going to stay with my aunt and uncle so she could stay in the same school. Mom then told me I'd have more free time and I could get a part time job to help out. I said sure. With the mood I had been in lately, walking on the beach sounded great to me. I could think about things, get my head straight.

Mary and her brothers, Curtis and Barney, helped us move. It was pretty cool living on the beach. I got a job at a drugstore, where I was a soda jerk and worked at the cosmetic counter as well. It was a pretty good job. School started and I didn't want to go to my new school. I had always gone to Terry Parker High School, and I wanted to graduate with my friends. Mom didn't make me register at Fletcher. I guess she was too busy and figured I'd get bored and change my mind.

I still only worked part time. The rest of the day I spent on the beach. I just couldn't get excited about anything. Mary would come over and spend the night on weekends. She'd say, "Girl, you've got to get back into the swing of things. You need to start going to the dances again and meet some guys. You need to start dating again! You need to get on with your life. I need that old Betty back." Mary stayed Friday and Saturday night, going home Sunday.

I was home reading a book Sunday night when someone knocked on the door. When I answered the door, I was shocked to see my old boyfriend, Jimmy Hall. I asked him how he had found me. He told me that Mary had called and told him I was going through a rough time with my family and she thought he would want to know where I was. Jim-

my said he hadn't tried to get in touch with me before because he thought I didn't want to see him after our breakup.
I told him I was glad to see him and asked him to come in.

Mom said hi to Jimmy. "Maybe you can get Mopey in a
better mood," she said. He laughed and we sat and talked.
He told me what he had been doing. He was in college and
was planning on going into the Army Reserve. I had really
missed him. We had dated about a year and a half and he
was with me when I found out my parents were planning on
getting a divorce. Now we seemed so far apart. I think it
was me. I felt almost guilty about what happened with Tug.
It's hard to explain. He asked if I would like to go out on
Friday night. I said sure and walked him to the door. He
gave me a goodnight kiss and left. I was happy and sad, if
you can understand. Here was a boy I had dated for a year.
We really did care about each other, but we were too young
to know whether we were in love or not. We had broken up
because he was going to college and he wanted to be free to
see other girls while he was away. He thought I should see
other guys, too. Why was he back? I thought we had broken
up for good. When a guy gives you that line about seeing
other people, to me it means it's an easy way for them to go
on in other directions. Now I was totally confused with life
in general.

If we decided we wanted to get back together, what was I
going to do? I had messed everything up. I was not the
same girl. I called good ole Mary. She said she'd get her
brother to bring her over Monday when she got out of
school.

When Mary came on Monday I told her about Jimmy
wanting to go out. She said, "That's great, Betty, then you
can start getting back to your old self."

"How can I?" I asked. "I'm not the same."

Jimmy Hall

Mary Jay Bryant

"Yes, you are! You're still Betty. You don't have to tell anyone what happened with Tug. Someday, when you meet the right guy, and you're sure, you'll know how to tell him. Then you can tell him the truth, if you want to. Betty, you're a pretty girl. You'll have lots of boyfriends before Mr. Right comes along. So you made a mistake, and it probably won't be the last one you ever make either. You will survive. And besides, we have our careers to look forward to. We're going to be dancers, remember?"

She made a lot of sense. I told her that I thought I was going to go back to school next month.

"Good," Mary said. "Everybody misses you!"

"I can catch up and maybe, after a few months, I can talk Mom into letting me go back to Parker."

The next week passed, and I was feeling much better about myself. Jimmy and I went to the show and for pizza with his usual gang (entourage). Come to think of it, we never went anywhere alone. We talked about getting back together. I told him maybe we would someday, but with him in college and now going into the Army Reserve, I didn't see much hope in it. We talked every few days. He would call from St. Petersburg where he was in school.

Mary and I went to the radio station. I hadn't worked there in a while because after we moved to the beach transportation was a problem. We wanted to see if any shows were coming up for us to dance at. There was a big one coming—The Rolling Stones. Sure, we wanted to dance at that one, but we probably couldn't because of that union dispute.

I told Mom I wanted to go back to school, and she was glad. I quit my job and was getting things back together. It was mid-September now, and while I was straightening up the house one day, I realized I hadn't started my period this month. I was never late and it was almost the third week in September. I always started on the first! I finished cleaning, fixed a Coke, and sat down to listen to the radio and write Mary a note. We always wrote notes as well as talking everyday. While I was writing, I just stopped. For some reason I started crying and I couldn't stop. I threw the notebook across the room. I knew I must be pregnant. Oh, God, what am I going to do? Why me? I know girls that have sex with their boyfriends all the time. Why did I have to be the one to get pregnant the first time? Then I thought, Well, I know girls who have missed their periods and not been pregnant. It'll be okay. I pushed the thought out of my mind. I said to myself, "Betty, you've got to think positive. It's all fine, everything is. Forget it!"

Chapter 4

About a week later, Dad came to see Mom. He said Johnny had stayed in Louisiana with Mom's older sister, Aunt Sis, and her family. We all had a short visit and I said I had to go visit my girlfriend. I could tell they wanted to talk. Dad was in a better mood: he seemed more mellow, calmer than he had been since the divorce. I left and picked up Mary. We picked up Joyce and Clara, and we all went to the movies and then cruising. I was going to start at Fletcher High School on the first of October. I was still hoping Mom would work it out for me to go back to Terry Parker. I could use Mary's home address, but transportation was going to be a problem.

When I got back home that night, Mom said she and Dad had had a long talk and had decided to get back together.

"Great! We can all move back into our old house and be a family again," I said.

"No," Mom said. "Your dad sold the house and his business. We're going to move to Louisiana." I just couldn't believe this was happening. She told me if I didn't want to go, we wouldn't, but just to think about it.

Well, that sure put the pressure on me. If I refused, she would use that as an excuse and Dad would blame me. He'd say it was my fault if they didn't get back together. I didn't know what to do; our family was in total disarray. Maybe I should go. I had my friends and Jimmy. What about us—if there was any us left? I thought about it all night. The next day I told her I would go.

Needless to say, I didn't enroll in school because we would be moving in the next few weeks. I called Mary; we had to work on a plan. We decided we would get an apartment together as soon as she got out of school. We would both get jobs. I would go to Louisiana and save up money so we would be able to put our plan into action.

I was busy packing while Mom worked getting ready for the move. It was now the first week of October and I was still patiently waiting for my period so that I could breathe easier and put the past year behind me. Another week passed. I knew I must be pregnant. It seemed like all I did anymore was cry. This was supposed to be my senior year—the best year of my life! What happened? What did I do that was so bad to deserve this?

It was morning and Mom had gone to work. I was supposed to finish packing for the move. I had tossed and turned all the previous night. I kept having nightmares about that day with Tug. How was I going to deal with this situation? I had to tell Mary. Maybe she could help me think this through. I kept wrapping plates awaiting 3:00 p.m., when Mary got out of school. What was I going to do? Mom and Dad would kill me!

At 3:30 p.m I could finally talk to Mary. "Mar, I'm pregnant," I told her.

"Oh no, Betty. I'm so sorry. Are you sure? Have you been to a doctor, yet?"

"No, but I'm sure."

"Are you going to call Tug?"

"Why?" I asked. "What's he going to do? Laugh at me and say, 'Too bad little girl.' No, I'm not going to tell him."

"Are you going to tell your Mom?" Mary asked.

"No! No one! And don't you tell anyone either!''

"Oh, Betty, you know I won't. Are you going to keep the baby?''

"Of course, that's the only thing I am sure of. I just can't believe all this is happening. I'm not even ready to be on my own yet. I've got one whole year of school left, and now I've got someone who will need me to take care of him or her.''

"So, what are you going to do?'' Mary questioned.

"I don't know. I guess I'll go to Louisiana to make sure my family gets back together, and as soon as I can, I'll save up money and we can still get an apartment together. But not here, and not in Louisiana. After I have the baby, it will be easier to break the news to Mom and Dad.''

Mary told me that her brother was a college professor and preacher who lived in Tallahassee. He and his wife would help us get jobs and an apartment. I could go to night school and get my diploma.

"You know, Mary, my baby will be born in May around our graduation time. That's ironic, isn't it?'' I said. "Instead of a diploma I'll get a baby''—I didn't cry; I guess I had run out of tears. I was glad we at least had a tentative plan.

It was going to be hard to leave Jacksonville. All my friends were there. I told Jimmy I was leaving and he told me he would come to visit as soon as he could, but I knew we'd probably never see each other again. That was a bad feeling, a kind of a kick in the stomach. We were supposed to leave in two days. As Mom and Dad went out to dinner, Mom said there was a letter for me on the table. It was an envelope from "Where the Action Is.'' I opened it and saw it was a confirmation for my audition with the television show. The audition was scheduled for February 12, 1967.

Well, that's just great! I thought. I'll be big and pregnant! I guess this will be one audition I don't make. All my dreams of what I had wanted were gone now. I had wanted to be a dancer, to go to college at Auburn. I had picked Auburn when I was just a freshman; I wanted to take business management. That way if I became the dancer I wanted to be I could handle the business side of my career as well. But now I had to worry about what would be best for my baby. I just hoped he or she would understand everything. Maybe someday I could even go back to school so my child would be proud of me. I didn't want him or her to grow up with a dropout for a mother. I had a person inside me that would need me, that would depend on me.

I couldn't believe all this could happen to just one person. I thought it must be a dream—no, a nightmare. I watched a little television and went to bed. Sleep was not easy. I kept waking up with the same nightmare and couldn't go back to sleep.

Finally, D-Day arrived and the moving van took all our stuff. Regina was back and the four of us headed for Louisiana. Usually on trips I sang all the way. This trip all I could do was stare out the window, wishing all this would disappear. It took twelve hours to get to my grandmother's house in Winnsboro, Louisiana. It was about 9 p.m when we arrived, and all my mom's family was there to greet us. It was like a family reunion; they had a big country meal waiting for us. We only saw my mom's family every couple of years when we'd visit for Thanksgiving, so we didn't know them well.

Dad already had a job with a television repair shop. Mom got a job at a beauty salon. We moved into a house in town. Mom and Dad kept trying to get me to register in school, but I kept telling them I wasn't ready. Mom would tell Dad not to push me. She knew I wasn't happy about the move, but that's all she knew. As time went by, I put in applications for jobs. I babysat neighbors' kids and my family. This country life sure was different. There was nothing to do, and there was only one movie house showing movies I had already seen. I had a cousin Gail, who was two years younger than I, and I used to visit her, but I felt so old around her and her friends. I liked going over to my cousin Sammie Pearl's house. She was five years older and had two kids. I got to babysit for her a lot and I enjoyed talking to her. I would help her with dinner when her husband worked late. My brother was still staying with my aunt. He wasn't ready to move back in yet. I think he wanted to be sure. He was comfortable at my aunt's. She had three girls and a younger boy, and they enjoyed Johnny. I think Johnny liked the attention—you know, the middle child syndrome. But soon the family would all be together again.

I wrote Mary every day. I would tell her about all the changes I was experiencing as my baby was growing inside of me. I still didn't know how I was going to get through all of this and how long I could keep my secret. I wrote my other girlfriends from time to time, but Mary and I kept in close touch. She sent me an article about Tug going to New York as a relief pitcher for the New York Mets. His career was growing, and so was my belly.

I had gained a little weight, but not much. Mom said something once about me finally putting on some weight—I had always been so thin. But it was easy to disguise the weight and size of my stomach. Smock tops were in, as were baby doll dresses. I never wore anything tight, but my face was getting a little puffy, and my feet were always swelling. My grandmother said it was all the country cooking that was making me look a little fuller, as she put it. It probably was her homemade biscuits. They were about all I ate.

They raised their own food, including eggs. Fresh eggs looked terrible. I just couldn't eat those dark orange yolks. The milk was fresh cow's milk and had cream floating on the top, I just could not drink it. The only other thing I liked was butter beans. We never had anything like that at home. The closest thing we had were lima beans. Everyone had big gardens in my family, and they all raised their own beef and hogs. Boy, was it ever a different life.

As time went by my cousins started trying to fix me up with different boys. I just pretended I was mourning for my old boyfriend so they would leave me alone. I had his picture on my dresser and wrote letters to him all the time.

Morning sickness wasn't too bad and didn't last for long. It was kind of hard to hide from my family, but I pretended I had the flu. By the end of January, trying to hold my stomach in got harder and harder. The baby was moving; it was a weird feeling, and I couldn't tell anybody. This should be a happy experience for a girl. I was turning into a woman and would soon be a mother. I did know one thing—I wanted my baby to know just how much I loved him or her and to know I would always be there for him or her. I also wondered how I would tell my child what really happened that August evening. I talked to my belly, my child, all the time. I would sing to this child. I wanted him or her to know what had happened wasn't his or her fault.

I wrote Mary and told her about all I was feeling. She kept wanting to know when I was leaving. I couldn't figure out how. I had managed to put up a little money and I thought I'd get a little more on my birthday in March. If I got enough money, I'd catch a bus out of here.

Mom always had a lot of family over. She invited my Aunt Clara Ann, Aunt Dink, Uncle Tommy, Sammie, and my grandparents for her famous spaghetti dinner one night.

She kept giving me strange looks. When everyone left, I did dishes and went to bed. The next morning, I heard Mom tell Dad she wasn't feeling well so she wasn't going to work. Dad took Regina to school. I was awake but still lying in bed. After Dad drove off, Mom called to me.

"Betty Ann, Betty Ann?" She always called me that when she was upset about something. I finally got up after the third "Betty Ann." I put on my housecoat and walked into the living room.

"Yes, ma'am," I said.

"Sit down," Mom said. I sat down and then she said, "All right, how far along are you?"

I was shocked, but I played dumb. "What do you mean?" I said.

"You're pregnant," she said, "and I want to know how long." I just looked at her and told her she was crazy. Then I started crying. After I had cried for a few minutes, I said, "I think I'm about six months."

"Have you told him?" she asked. I shook my head no. Mom hugged me and headed for the phone. I asked her what she was doing and she said she was calling Jimmy to tell him. She said that he needed to know and that we had dated for over a year so we'd get married and work this out.

I couldn't believe this. I started crying harder and said, "Please, Mom, hang up the phone. Jimmy will think you've lost your mind. We haven't done anything."

"Well, who then?" she asked. I just looked at her and she looked at me and said, "That damned Tug McGraw! I told you he was too old for you!" She exploded. She went on and on. When she had finally finished, she said we would have to call him.

I refused and told her, "Absolutely not! I never want to see or talk to him again."

"So, what are you going to do? This is just as much his responsibility as it is yours," Mom said. I then told her about the plan Mary and I had come up with.

"No, Betty. This is my grandchild and I want to be there when this baby is born. You've got to let me call Tug. If you and Tug don't get married, the birth certificate will say illegitimate (as was still the custom in the 1960s). Do you want your child going through life with that? People will be calling him a little bastard. You need to think about this, Betty Ann. Put your pride aside. It's not just your problem; it's Tug's problem, too."

"Mom, I can't call him. I'm too embarrassed, and he'll just laugh at me. He doesn't care. He'll think I'm just stupid. I hardly knew him. It happened. I don't want him to know. I'll take care of this baby myself."

Mom told me to think about it. "You've got to do what's best for your baby. Put your pride aside and think about the baby. You can't worry about your feelings, Tug's feelings, or anyone else's. You have to do what's best for your baby." With that statement, she called New York. She left a message with the Mets office to have Tug call her.

Chapter 5

That evening, Mom told me she needed help to tell my dad, because he was not going to take this too well. You have to remember I come from an Italian Catholic background and this was not going to sit well with my dad. Mom called her brother, Uncle Buddy. He and Aunt Margie came over to discuss all this with Mom. Aunt Margie was so nice to me. She took me into the bedroom and talked to me, asking questions about the baby, such as was it moving, how was I feeling. It made me happy and sad. Happy that I was finally able to talk to someone about the life growing inside me. The changes my body was going through were so amazing. Aunt Margie was wonderful. She never said anything about Tug or the situation. We just talked about babies.

My mom's brother left to go and tell my father in an attempt to have him calmed down before he came home. Mom started asking me if I wanted to tell my grandparents. I told her no. I was too embarrassed. I still couldn't believe it had happened in the first place. I finally agreed to let my mom and Aunt Margie tell my grandparents the whole story. Mom said I would see that my family would rally around me and come to my aid.

Dad and Uncle Buddy came home late. Uncle Buddy decided that he and Aunt Margie would spend the night to help keep the peace. My dad was known to have quite a temper, and they wanted to be there to help Mom. Although I knew my dad wouldn't physically hurt me, he would be upset. Dad came in the door yelling at my mother, telling her that she knew I was pregnant all along and that was the only reason she decided to get back together with him. He thought it was a plot against him. They argued for a long time. Finally, I came out of my room and told him that no one had known and that he would not have to take care of my baby—I was going to do that!

All he could say was, "Yeah, sure. And how do you think you're going to do that? You're going to call that damn Tug McGraw. He's making money, and he's going to pay you some money to help support that baby."

I ran crying to my room. As I lay on the bed crying, I remembered what my mother had said. It made sense. This was Tug's responsibility. Why should my child grow up without a father, be called names, and be made fun of? But how do you live with someone you don't even know? I didn't know what I should do. Wouldn't a child be better off with someone who really wanted it and loved it. How did I know that Tug even wanted it? I didn't know if Tug cared anything about me. I finally cried myself to sleep.

The next morning Mom made me a doctor's appointment. She, Aunt Margie, and I went to see the doctor. We explained to him that I was about six months pregnant and I never had an examination, and wasn't married. He gave me a thorough examination and told me to come back the following week when he would give me my expected date of delivery. He discussed money with Mom.

The baby would be born at the clinic and the bill would be about five hundred dollars. We would have to come up with some money since I didn't have any insurance to cover this pregnancy. We stopped for ice cream after leaving the doctor's office. Mom said we would go over to my grand-parents and tell them what was going on. I told the two of them to just take me home; they could tell my grandparents. They took me home and I went to my room and started writing Mary a letter.

Right after Mom came back at around 2 p.m., the phone rang. Mom answered; it was Tug. All I could hear was her side of the conversation. She had to fill me in later. She said to Tug, "I guess you know I'm Betty's mom." He answered that he did, and wanted to know where I was and how I was. She informed him that we had moved to Louisiana. He said he had wondered what had happened to me, that when he left for New York, he had tried to find me to tell me good-bye. Mom stopped him and said, "Tug, I guess you know why I'm calling."

"No, I have no idea," he said.

"Betty's pregnant," she said.

He didn't say anything for a while, then he said, "So, why are you calling me?"

"Well, Tug, it was her first time, and you were the only one."

He didn't say anything at first, then tried to deny it. "No! It's not mine!"

Mom said, "Tug, most guys can tell when it's the first time with a girl and you should have been able to tell that she was a virgin!" Mom said.

He finally said, "Yeah. What do you want me to do?"

"I want you and Betty to get married."

'I don't know about that"

"You don't have to live together. Just get married for the baby."

"I have to talk to my father, I'll call you back."

As Mom hung up the phone, Dad came in. He wanted to

know who she was talking to. When she told him, he wanted to know if Mom had asked Tug for money. I started yelling, "I don't want any money for the baby! And, if you ask him for any money, I'll leave here and you'll never see me or my baby again!" I ran to my room crying. I had my pride. If he didn't want us, I didn't want anything from him. I could do it by myself. I certainly didn't need his pity.

That evening, my grandparents came over to see me. Everyone was really nice; my grandfather handed me two hundred dollars and told me to take this money to the doctor when I went back to him. I thanked him and told him I didn't want to take his money, that I could get a job and raise the money myself. He said, "Betty, you can't get a job until after you have your baby, so take the money and when you get a job, you can pay me back." He was so sweet. He never asked me anything about Tug.

My grandparents were terrific. This was a lot of money to them. They weren't the type to throw money around. They had a small farm and lived in a farmhouse that didn't have indoor plumbing for a long time. It was very special to me that they wanted to help me and my baby.

My Aunt Clara Ann also came over; she was always so good to me. Aunt Clara, Sammie Pearl, and I were very close. We talked about babies and I had a chance to tell someone, other than Mary, what was happening to me. Only one person in the family ever said anything negative — a cousin told me I was going to ruin my life by having this baby and that I shouldn't consider keeping it at all. She said the baby would be better off with a mother and a father. She also said that I would miss out on everything in life: college, career. Right! I hadn't even finished high school yet! She wouldn't let up. She kept insisting I give my baby up. I finally told her to leave me alone and went to my room.

I couldn't even think about giving my baby up. Maybe it would be right for someone else, but not me. This was my child no matter what the circumstances. I loved this baby already. I wanted to see it grow up and I wanted to be there for this child. I do realize though that my cousin was trying to help.

When I went back to the doctor, he told me the baby would be born about May 7. He said I was in fairly good health for someone who had no prenatal care. He did tell me I was a little anemic and put me on iron pills and told me not to gain much weight. I hadn't yet and I didn't think that would be a problem. I weighed 105 at his office. I was wrong: I began putting on weight. I guess I was more relaxed now that everyone knew and was eating better. I wasn't having to hold my stomach in any longer, since I didn't have to worry about hiding anymore. (Still, since I was so thin, I weighed only 115 pounds when the baby was born.)

On my birthday, we had a party, which became a baby shower. I got everything I would need: diapers, shirts, gowns, bottles. My mother gave me baby dresses, because she wanted a granddaughter. I wanted a boy and wanted him to look just like Tug McGraw. Tug was a handsome man, and I wanted my son to be just as handsome. I wanted my son to be strong, handsome, and intelligent. I wanted him to grow up to be "somebody" just to show Tug McGraw. I would pray for God to make him special, someone who would be more caring than his father was in this circumstance. I wanted him just to be a stronger person and to know that he was loved.

A few days after my birthday, Mom got a call from Tug. He told her that he had talked to his father, his older brother, and his manager, and they all advised him to deny everything. He was told that since his career was just starting, something like this could ruin everything. Mom got mad and told him he was going to be sorry for denying his child. He told her he didn't care and not to ever contact him again. Ever! Mom hung up the phone and told me what he had said.

"Fine," I told her. I can't make him care about me. I can't make him care about his baby. If that's what he wants, fine. It will be my baby. He will have no say-so about my baby. I can take care of it, Mom. I don't want my child to have a father, even if it's in name only, if he doesn't want him." She said the least Tug could do was to give my baby a last name. She said either that or she and my dad would adopt the baby.

"No!" I yelled. "No one is going to adopt my baby! I'm tired of people telling me I need to give my baby up. This is my baby. I'm going to keep it. I'm going to raise it. If it bothers you that my baby does not have a father, I'll go away. I can go stay with Mary."

"No, no," she said. "We'll give the baby Tug's last name."

I can remember trips to the store. I felt like everyone was looking at me, like they knew I wasn't married. I guess it was stupid, but I felt that way—that everyone thought I was an awful person, pregnant and no husband. Mom kept getting things ready for her "granddaughter." She keep buying pink things. And every night I prayed for a healthy baby. But I also prayed that this child would be a boy and be somebody special that everyone would love. I wanted my baby to have a lot of love to make up for not having a father.

Regina was excited about being an aunt. My brother Johnny was still living at my mom's sister's. He didn't want to move back home. I missed him but I had enough problems of my own. (He never did move back with us. The year after Tim was born, Johnny was drafted and went to VietNam. We wrote when we could to each other, and when he got out of the Army, he moved to Texarkana and has been there ever since.)

In April, my grandparents were working their garden. They were also picking blackberries and dewberries. I had no idea what dewberries were. I came to find out that they were similar to blackberries. We made pies and jams. Everything was going well. We had moved to the country to a little brown house in a place called The Crossroads. Daddy, my grandfather, and my uncle had built my mom a beauty shop in the house so that after the baby came, she could help watch the baby when I got a job. We had a good day with my grandparents, aunt, and uncle.

Later that evening, I woke up not feeling very well. My stomach was hurting a little, so I made myself a cup of cocoa and sat in the rocker to drink it. Mom got up and wanted to know what was wrong. I told her I just didn't feel very well. She wanted to know if I was hurting, and I told her just a little. Mom was so nervous; this was her first grandchild. (It seemed funny since she had three children of her own.)

Mom said we were going to the hospital. My doctor wasn't on duty, but another doctor was. He was very rough when he examined me. He really hurt me. Remember, I had only had sex one time. He got so rough, I started bleeding. It really began hurting then. I hurt all day long. Finally, he ordered the nurse to give me a shot to help with the pain. I was hurting so bad, all I could do was cry. My doctor came in the next evening. I had been in labor for twelve hours, but I wasn't contracting like I was supposed to do. My doctor got mad at the first doctor for giving me the shot. He said it wasn't allowing my labor to progress properly, and after 18 hours the doctor said it was time for me to have my baby. I'm a strong woman. I can normally tolerate pain, but the pain and the emotional state I was in made my labor intolerable. I was crying and calling for my mother.

Finally, the baby was coming. I knew hardly anything about having a baby. The doctor explained as he did things. He said, "Now we are going to break your water."

I said, "I don't care. I don't want it." I didn't know what he was talking about. And when he talked about dilating in centimeters, I didn't know what that meant either. I was a naive 18 year-old. I think that's why I made sure I talked with my children about everything. With life changing, parents need even more communication with their children. This changes with each generation.

After 18 hours of labor, my baby was born. The doctor told me I had a boy. I was ecstatic! But soon I started crying again, because I knew my mother was going to be disappointed, since she wanted a girl. I was worried that no one was going to love my baby but me, because of the circumstances, and now I was disappointing my mother by having a boy. But my mom was happy as could be. Her first grandchild. She thought he was terrific and still does.

Mom called Tug and told him he had a son. He didn't want to know anything about the baby, but he did ask if I was all right. Mom told him I had a hard delivery, but I was fine. I asked her if he was coming to the hospital. I then said I didn't think I could stand seeing him. She assured me that there was no chance of that happening.

The next morning, we filled out the birth certificate. I had decided that I wanted to name my son after my mom's dad, who had died when she was a young girl. But I wanted

House where Betty lived when Tim was born

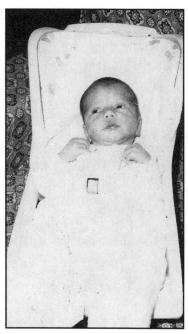

Betty in 1967

Tim one week old

to make sure it would be all right with her stepfather first,
so I called him. Since it didn't bother him, I named my son,
born May 1, 1967, Samuel Timothy McGraw, and I signed
the birth certificate. Well, we had used the name McGraw
and the doctor never asked any questions. We were in the
hospital for five days. I was getting anxious to get home
with my baby.

Timmy and I got ready to leave the hospital. He was the
prettiest baby I had ever seen. Lots of black hair, olive com-
pletion and big black eyes. The nurses told me they had
never seen so much hair on a baby. They made a curl on top
of his head. But I combed the curl out and combed his hair
to the side. I wanted my baby to look like a boy. Timmy
was beautiful.

When we got home everyone was there to greet us. Most
everyone was very good to me; they were all good to Timmy. Just a few had things to say about me not being married. Of course, everyone wanted to hold him. I could tell
right away he was going to be spoiled. Paw-Paw, my grandfather, came into my room and looked at Tim in his bed. He
then laid two hundred dollars beside him. I said, "No, Paw-
Paw. You already paid some of the bill at the hospital." He
said he wanted me to buy this baby something with the
money and let him know how much we all loved him. I
cried and hugged Paw-Paw. He was wonderful to me and
Timmy. I took the money and paid on the rest of my hospital bill. Tim didn't need anything, and I needed to pay the
hospital.

The next day, I walked to the mailbox (it was just a little
way down from the driveway). I had a letter from Mary. I
needed to write to her and tell her about my beautiful son. I
was so proud of him—he's just perfect! I wanted to give
her all the details of the long day and of Timmy's birth.

Mary's letter was all about graduation. They had had a big party. Everyone asked her if she had heard from me. She told them I was great and getting ready for my graduation and college. No one except Mary knew the truth. But I didn't care. I had my baby. It was a little depressing at the time, hearing about everyone. I missed my friends. But really, I wouldn't have given my baby up for anything. I loved him very much. He was worth all the bad times.

Mom and Dad still weren't getting along. They argued a lot and when they weren't arguing, they weren't speaking. About a week after Tim was born, I got my first letter from my old boyfriend. He said he and his friends were going to come visit. They were going to Texas and were planning on seeing me on their drive there. My Aunt Clara Ann and I talked about it. Since he knew nothing about my baby, I needed to write and tell him. I did and explained everything. Needless to say, letters from him stopped coming quickly.

I would lie in bed at night just looking at Timmy. He was so small and precious. I'd pray for God to bless him. Let him grow up and be someone special and make something of himself someday. Maybe his dad would regret what he missed by not watching his son grow up. I guess like everyone, I dreamed that my knight in shining armor would come carry us away and take care of us. Sometimes it was even Tug in my dreams, and he'd say how much he wanted Timmy in his life. I guess everyone needs dreams, even though they rarely do come true.

The clinic where Tim was born

The bus station cafe where Betty worked

Chapter 6

Time passed and I got a part-time job at the garment factory. Mom and Dad finally split for good and he went to Texarkana. We were on our own again. Mom's shop was in the house now. I still missed my friends in Florida, but I liked being a Mommy to my little boy. I wasn't making much money and I needed to help Mom with the rent and car, so I got another part-time job waiting tables two nights a week at the local cafe. Tips weren't great, but it helped. Mom made a couple of friends in the next town about thirty miles away and would go to a club there. She and I went a couple of times together. It felt strange to dance again. I just felt so old, and I didn't like leaving Tim with a babysitter.

Mom accepted a job offer to teach beauty school in Rayville, Louisiana. The bus station cafe there needed someone full time, so Mom wanted us to move. I took the job at the bus station and earned forty-five dollars per week, more than I was making from both my part-time jobs. From time to time, they even let me bring Tim's playpen with me. We rented a house that cost us sixty-five dollars per month, not much more than the fifty-five dollars we had been paying. It was an old house made into four apartments; we had one bedroom with a bathroom in it; no walls separated the bathroom. With my half of expenses plus babysitters and groceries, I would have five dollars a week left over for extras like Tim's doctor bills and personal items.

Sometimes I would have to pull a double shift if someone didn't show up for work. It meant more money, but trying to get Tim situated was hard. He was really a good
baby, though, which made things easier for me. I had to take
him off his formula because I couldn't afford it. I asked the
free clinic if I could use whole milk yet. They told me no,
but said I could use Carnation with water and corn syrup.
The only baby food he liked was applesauce. He loved
scrambled eggs and grits, mashed potatoes and green beans.

Mom went out of town a lot so I'd have to leave Tim
with a sitter. He would cry, and so would I. I never had any
extra money, but it didn't matter. I was so happy with my
baby. My dad came to see my sister and me occasionally.
My brother was still at my aunt's. He had quit school and
was working, so we didn't see much of him.

We decided that Regina should stay with Maw-Maw for a
little while. It was hard on her with Mom working all the
time, and I had to work a lot too. It wasn't fair to her to
have to watch Timmy so much. I sure missed having her
around; she was a big help with Timmy. But she was only
12 and needed to be with kids her own age. We had cousins
around Maw-Maw's; she didn't have any friends in Rayville.

I had made a friend at the garment factory who lived in
Rayville, and she came to visit every now and then. Her
name was Judy and she was great; her mom was a very
sweet person. She invited me and Timmy over for dinner a
lot and even babysat if Judy and I wanted to go somewhere,
as long as we didn't stay too late. We went out sometimes
when I could get a day off. We would drive to Monroe,
which was a bigger town where there were things to do.

I followed Tug's career in the papers. He was doing
great. They said he was making everyone see what a relief
pitcher was. I was proud of him for his career, but angry

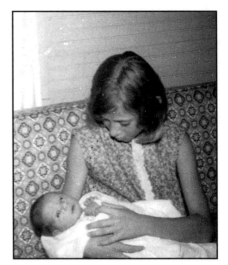

Regina holding Tim at
15 days old

Infant Tim

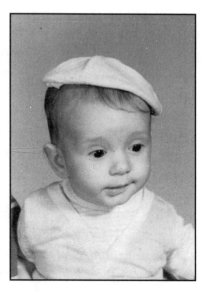

too. It was very hard taking care of Timmy by myself. I wanted to give him everything. I just wished Tug cared for him.

Working at the cafe meant meeting a lot of people. It wasn't big, but it was where everyone had coffee and lunch. Lunch was the busiest time of day. All the farmers and their hands ate there. There was only one other restaurant and one lounge that served sandwiches. One big, loud-talking guy came in all the time. You know the type, the one who always gives the waitresses a hard time. His name was Horace Smith. He was big, six feet tall and over 200 pounds. He came in a lot with another guy my mom had gone out with a few times. Every time I'd end up waiting on his table, he always asked me when I was going to take him away from all of this. He was a lot older than I (11 years) and anytime I had Timmy with me, he would just take him out of my arms and play with him. Timmy loved it! He loved the attention people gave him.

Horace was always asking me out. One night Mom said, "Why don't you go out with him?" When I told her he was too old, she said that my dad was 12 years older than her. She said an older man would take care of me and Timmy. One day at work he was bugging me again to go out with him in front of a group of his friends. I just said okay and told him to pick me up at seven. He nearly fell out of his chair. I don't think he expected me to take him up on it. I figured maybe Mom was right. Also I didn't think any boy my age was going to be interested in me, since I had a baby. So why not go out with Horace; he seemed nice enough.

All I had ever saw him drive was an old pickup truck. It was a surprise when he drove up in a pretty white car (that belonged to his sister) and all dressed up to boot! We went to dinner at the Magnolia Restaurant and later danced in the lounge in the back. He was a good dancer for such a big guy. He took me back to my apartment at about 11 p.m. As he walked me to the door he asked for another date. I told him I would think about it, and thanked him for the evening.

I went inside to check on Timmy. He and my mom were fast asleep. It was time for him to wake up for a bottle. He hadn't quite gotten to the point that he was sleeping all night, although sometimes he would. I changed Tim, fed him, and we both fell asleep in the rocking chair. When I woke up at 4 a.m. to go to work, I put Tim in his crib. Mom got up later than I did so she took Tim to the sitter for me. Then she would usually come by for coffee before going in to the beauty school.

She came in that morning and asked about my date, I told her it was fun, that we had gone to dinner and dancing. I really missed dancing a lot.

Horace came in for lunch and asked to take Timmy and me to dinner. I told him that I would be able to go on Saturday, and he said, "That's great!" I got off at noon and picked Timmy up from the sitter. We went for a walk. Someone had given me a stroller, and I took Timmy for walks almost every day. He loved it! He would look at everything, his big brown eyes always taking in the sights. He was growing so fast it was hard keeping him in clothes. I guess I never realized how fast kids grew. I bought most of his clothes at the Dollar Store and made most of mine.

I fixed dinner when we got home, and then we sat on the sofa and watched a little TV. Usually we would rock in the rocking chair, and I would sing. Timmy liked for me to sing to him. Every night after his bath I'd rock him to sleep singing to him. "My Fair Lady" was my favorite musical, and I knew the soundtrack backward and forward. Timmy loved those songs. (I could remember riding around in the car with Mary and singing "Loverly," and now I was singing it to my baby!) Timmy heard a mixture of music from musicals to George and Tammy, Dolly and Porter, the Beach Boys, The Beatles, and even Tommy Dorsey. I had a big collection of albums. Timmy always liked Elvis; he would bounce every time he heard him, just like he knew each time it was Elvis.

I knew he would walk early because he was always trying. He didn't like sitting; he always wanted to stand in your lap. Timmy was about five and a half months old now and getting cuter every day. We didn't have much—actually we didn't have anything—but we were happy. I wouldn't have traded places with anybody. I loved my little boy so much.

Horace and I went out a few more times, and every Sunday he'd show up at my door. He knew I did laundry on Sunday, so he would bring his laundry also and do it at the laundromat while I did mine. He would always go get ice cream and feed it to Timmy. Timmy was in a walker and into everything by then; he would have chocolate ice cream all over his face.

One day Horace said, " Betty, you ought to marry me. I need a wife and a family. I'm 30 years old and need someone to be responsible for. You could quit work and stay home with Timmy all day. You work too hard, and you're missing a lot of time with Timmy."

"I don't know," I said. "We don't even know each other. You should be in love when you marry someone."

"Well just think about it," Horace said. I did, especially as I started my work day.

At 4 a.m. the next morning, it was time for me to go to work again. Mom wasn't home so I had to take Timmy with me until the sitter would keep him at 8 a.m. He was always

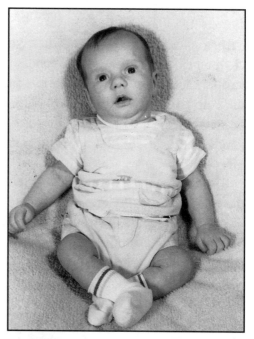

Tim 3 months

Tim

such a cheerful baby, even when you woke him up. It was November and quite cold. I bundled him up, pulled out the stroller, and we walked to work. I put him in the playpen at the cafe and started the coffee. Timmy was wide awake and pointed to the jukebox wanting me to put money into it. I laughed; it was 5:30 in the morning and he was wanting music.

Horace came in, got a cup of coffee, and put money in the jukebox. Timmy started bouncing and getting louder to the music. I guess he thought he was entertaining. I only had about six customers for breakfast. Horace left and said he'd be back for lunch. The cook had come in, so at about 8:00 I left to take Timmy to the sitter. I went back to work. The other girl didn't show up so that meant I would have to pull a double shift. I called the sitter, and she said she would keep Timmy till I could get away. Now all I needed was energy! I was always tired.

The last time I had gone to the doctor I was still anemic, but since then I had been taking iron tablets. I sat down and ate a sandwich. I always ate like a bird and still only weighed 96 pounds. The second shift never was very busy, so time went by slowly. I needed to pick Timmy up by 4 p.m. and bring him back to the cafe until I got off work, which would be around 8 p.m.

Around 3:45 p.m. Horace came in with his buddies. He drove a gravel truck and did some farming for a guy in town. I guess he was the type that could do a little of everything. He told me he would go pick Tim up for me. I thanked him and said no, I would walk over and get him. He insisted. I agreed finally. It seemed to take him forever, I was beginning to worry when they arrived. They came in carrying a toy dump truck. Horace had stopped at the TG&Y store and bought it for Timmy. When 8 p.m. arrived

I was beat and ready to go home. I was putting Timmy's coat on as Horace came in the door. He offered to drive Timmy and me home. I thanked him and accepted the ride. I was ready to leave. When we got to my apartment, I offered to make some coffee. He said, "See how tired you are. Let's get married. I'll take care of you."

"Yes, I'm tired, so go home so I can go to sleep," I said.

At the end of the week Horace came by and wanted to go out. I said I couldn't because I was going to see my grandmother and sister. He asked if he could go. I said no, maybe next time. He continued to pressure me, but when he saw I wasn't going to give in, he finally left. We weren't a couple; we only went out. I wasn't ready to take someone to meet my family. I went to Maw-Maws with my Mom to see Regina. I told Regina about Horace bugging me to marry him. She asked me if I liked him. I said, "Yes, he's nice."

"I don't see what the problem is if you like him," she said.

"But Regina, I don't love him. I just like him," I said, "Just drop the subject. I don't know why I'm talking to you about it anyway; you're only 11." We went in the other room, where my mom and grandmother were.

I always liked going to Maw-Maw's. She always loaded us up with fresh vegetables, which sure helped out. Aunt Clara Ann would always have a new outfit for Timmy. When I got home I sat down and wrote Mary a letter. I hadn't had time in a while to write to her, and I hadn't heard from her lately. A couple of days later I got a letter and a newspaper clipping from Mary. It was about Tug. It said he was getting married. I sat down just staring at the article. Timmy wasn't even a year old yet, and now he was getting married. He had said before Timmy was born that marriage would hurt his career. I guess it was kind of a shock. Maybe way back in my mind I thought Tug would show up one day, saying how sorry he was and want to take Timmy and me away from all this. Now it was evident he didn't care at all.

The next Thursday night Horace took me, Timmy, Mom, and her friend to dinner. Horace told Mom he wanted to marry me. I nearly choked! I couldn't believe he did that. I could hardly believe it when Mom told him she thought that was a great idea. He said if I married him my little sister could live with us. He even said he would adopt Timmy. By the end of the evening I had agreed, but not to Horace adopting Timmy. I decided that when Timmy was old enough, I was going to tell him about his real dad. I also told him that I wouldn't promise we'd stay together, but that I would try. My mom was excited; I think she just wanted someone to take care of me and Timmy.

We decided to get married the next week. We got the license, and I bought a new dress. My aunt kept Timmy for the weekend, and we got married. Horace's mom and sisters and my mom and sister were at the wedding. Horace's sister Barbara let us use her car for the weekend honeymoon to Monroe, so we wouldn't have to use the old truck. Mom told us we could keep the little apartment since she was moving in with her friend Joyce. I still had mixed emotions. Was I doing the right thing? Were we moving too fast? Then I'd tell myself I was doing the right thing. Horace needed me and wanted to take care of us. Regina would be back and we'd have a home life again. So this was right!

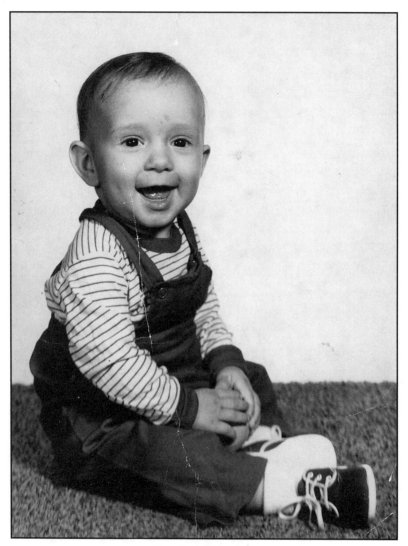

Tim at age 6 months

Chapter 7

When we returned from our weekend honeymoon, we picked up Timmy and Regina. I quit my job the following week and enrolled Regina in school. It seemed like we were a family again. Horace went to work, and I kept house and spent time with my baby. I could cook but because my dad was a city boy the things I had learned to cook were different from what Horace liked. He liked peas, cornbread, rice, steak, and gravy. Needless to say, I learned Southern cooking. I tried biscuits, but wasn't good at that so I had to use canned. He fussed but got used to it. By the time we were on our third week, things were going pretty well. It was crowded in the little apartment and Timmy was having a hard time adjusting to not sleeping with me. Horace wouldn't let him sleep in the bed with us. We had put him in a crib in the living room, and Regina slept on the couch.

One evening, Horace came home in a grouchy mood. He bit everyone's head off. I asked him what was wrong, and he snapped at me to shut up. It scared me and Regina, so we kept quiet. After dinner, we took Timmy out to play, so he wouldn't be noisy and make Horace mad. We came in and I gave Timmy his bath and rocked him to sleep. We all went to bed at 9 p.m.

Around 11, Timmy woke up crying. I got up to fix a bottle and change his diaper. While I was fixing his bottle, Horace got up. Instead of just crying, Timmy was now screaming. I went in to check on him and found Horace beating him for crying. He was spanking him like a grown kid, not a seven-month old. I screamed at Horace and told him to put Timmy down. He dropped Timmy in the crib and knocked me across the room with his fist. Regina grabbed Timmy and ran. Horace just went and got back into bed. I picked myself up from the floor, washed my face, and went outside to find my baby. He and Regina were sitting curled up on the front porch in a corner. We were all crying and scared. Regina asked, "What are you going to do?"

"We'll sit here and after he goes to sleep, we'll go in and sleep on the floor in the living room," I said.

When the alarm went off, I was still awake. I didn't know what would happen, so I just lay there afraid of what he might do. When Horace got up, he just got dressed and left. He never apologized or said a word; he just got dressed and left. I took a deep breath and tried to go back to sleep. I dozed off and on and finally got up. Regina went to school, and I gave the house a good cleaning. I picked flowers out of the yard and fixed a great dinner. Horace liked to eat as soon as he came in at 5:15 p.m. I didn't know what else to do. I thought maybe it had been my fault, that I shouldn't have yelled at him, but I couldn't watch him hurt my baby. I had a big black eye; I tried putting make-up on it, but it didn't help.

When Horace arrived at 5:15, Regina and I were terrified. He came in, went over to the playpen and rubbed Timmy on the head, and went to wash up. We sat down to eat without saying a word. Horace said, "Don't cook tomorrow. We are all going out to eat." I couldn't believe it. I had this awful black eye and he wanted to go out. Nothing was ever mentioned about him hitting me or Timmy.

The next night, we all went out to dinner. My mom's

friend Joyce was at the restaurant and asked what happened to my eye. I didn't say anything, and Horace said, "The dummy ran into the door." After we ate, we went home, watched some television, and went to bed. The next morning was Saturday, and someone came banging on the door and woke us up. I opened the door and found my mom there. She was really mad, she turned my head, looked at my face, and ran into the bedroom where she jumped on top of Horace. She began hitting him in the face. "You son-of-a-bitch! Let's see how you like it!"

Horace yelled for me to get her off of him. I pulled on her arm and finally she stopped. We went outside and she told me to get my stuff. I refused. I said, "Mom, I've got to try and make this work. Timmy and Regina need a home life." She yelled and told Horace she would kill him if he ever touched me again.

She left and I fixed breakfast. I took Horace a cup of coffee, and he warned me to keep my mother away from him. I didn't say anything. I didn't want to argue and have things get out of hand like they did the other night. Horace left to ride horses. He worked all week, and his weekends were spent roping cows and riding horses with his friends. Regina, Timmy, and I would just hang around the house or go to the school yard where they would play on the swings.

One day while Timmy and I were out walking, we saw another house down the street with an apartment for rent; it was bigger than the one we lived in. This one had two bedrooms and a bigger kitchen. The rent was a little more than we were currently paying. Horace earned a hundred dollars a week, but he was supposed to get a raise in a couple of months. He returned late that night and promised to check on the apartment.

Several weeks passed and I had not begun my period yet.

I assumed I was pregnant. I went to the local free clinic and, sure enough, I was. I was frightened. I didn't know how Horace would react. This would be another person to take care of. When Horace came home that night I told him. He was excited. "I hope it's a girl," I said.

"Nope," Horace said. "We're having a boy. We'll have all boys."

He got us the bigger apartment, and we moved in. We got another bed from his sister, and she bought me a washing machine. She rightfully assumed that since there would now be two babies, we would need it. Horace's sister Barbara and her husband, Dee, were always good to me and my baby. They would come by and get Timmy and take him for a Sunday drive with them. They never in all the years Horace and I were married showed any difference between our kids and Timmy.

Chapter 8

Horace had another sister in Winnsboro who was the complete opposite of Barbara. She never liked me or Timmy and never hesitated to show it. Horace's little sister, Charlotte, was about three years younger than I, and we got along very well. We became great friends and still are. He had another sister, Wilma, who lived far away. I never really got to know her too well, but we did get along. And his mother, Estelle, was wonderful.

Horace was a loud, grouchy person. He yelled at Timmy a lot and spanked him a little too often for trivial things. I believe in discipline, but Timmy was just a baby. Horace had an explosive temper; he was always mad about something. He didn't always hit us, but he did throw and break things often.

One evening, Horace was late coming home. He was a demanding person and wanted to be waited on hand and foot. I had dinner ready at the normal time. Finally at 6 p.m. I fed Regina and Timmy; after dinner, they went into the bedroom to color in a book. Timmy was 11 months old and walking and talking well. Horace came in around 7. I asked where he had been. "The god-damn pool hall with Claude!" I could tell he had been drinking. I never drank, but it didn't bother me that he did, although he became very mean when he drank. He yelled, "Where's my god-damn dinner?" He went into the kitchen and started throwing things around. "This shit is cold!"

I ran in and said, "If you'll sit down, I'll warm it up and fix you a plate." He kept screaming and knocked me down. I got up and went toward the bedroom. He yelled for me to come back to the kitchen and clean up the mess. Then he came at me. Timmy came out of the bedroom in his walker with his big brown eyes looking scared to death. I yelled for Regina to get him and take him outside.

At that moment, Horace hit me in the back of the head and I fell to the floor. I just lay there pretending I was unconscious so he would leave me alone. Horace left the house and Regina returned with Timmy. She helped me clean up the mess Horace had made. We didn't say anything. My neighbor knocked on the door asking if we were all right. I told her everything was okay and thanked her for checking on me. She knew Horace's sister Barbara and I felt sure she was going to say something to her. She did.

The next day, Barbara came by and asked me about it. I told her that Horace had just had too much to drink and that everything would be fine. I didn't mention to her the time before when he hadn't been drinking. She made me go to the doctor to make sure the baby and I were okay. We were. I had no physical marks this time, just a sick feeling inside. Horace again acted like nothing had happened. I wondered if he even remembered what he did when he would lose his temper. No one knew Horace was capable of anything like this. Everyone liked him. He was the type that never met a stranger, and I was sure this would never happen again. Plus, I was going to have two children now; maybe when he had one of his own things would be better.

Several months passed, and then Horace and his boss went to Texas to pick cotton. They were to be gone for two months but home every other weekend. We didn't have a car, so I wasn't able to go anywhere. My grandparents and

Tim, 19 months and Tracey, 3 months

relatives lived about thirty-five miles away, and Mom lived on the other side of town. I didn't see her often. Since we had no phone, I just hung around the house.

One weekend when Horace was away, Regina, Timmy and I went on a picnic at a wooded area about two miles from our house. We walked. We walked everywhere. The picnic area had a little stream. Tim played ball and enjoyed the water, and I painted the scenery. We were enjoying the day when Horace showed up. He said he really missed us. He wanted to visit the relatives, so we went to my Maw-Maw's and to see his Aunt Margaret on Sunday. We returned home around 3 p.m. so Horace could rest before he returned to Texas at midnight.

Around 8 p.m. I started having contractions. Horace called his sister, and they took me to the hospital. Her daughter stayed with Timmy and Regina. When we got to the hospital, Horace told the nurse that I was in labor. The nurse didn't believe him. She said, "You aren't big enough to be ready for delivery!" She weighed me and I weighed only 111 pounds. It was September 9, 1968, and Tracey Catherine Smith was born. She was so tiny, weighing six pounds and four ounces, with big brown eyes and lots of black hair . . . just like Timmy. She was a little fairer in complexion but absolutely perfect. Horace left that Monday night to return to work.

At the end of the week, Tracey and I went home. My mom came to help with the baby for a couple of days. When she left, Horace's sister, Charlotte, came to stay until he got back. I was having a harder time getting my strength back than I had with Timmy. I was very anemic, and so was Tracey. We were both given vitamins and iron.

Timmy was excited to have a baby sister. He liked being a big brother. He wanted to feed her all the time and help bathe and dress her. I would rock her, and he would sit on the arm of the rocking chair and sing to her. He'd sing "Rock-a-bye Baby" and Elvis's "Teddy Bear."

Horace returned from Texas and was home all the time. We moved from the apartment into a small house not far from his boss. The house had a yard where we put up swings for Timmy to play on outside. He was such a good child. All I ever had to do was mark off an imaginary line and tell him not to cross it and he wouldn't. He would play outside all morning. I would put Tracey in the playpen in the back yard while I hung up clothes.

Friends were nonexistent now. With no transportation, no phone and two babies, I stayed home all the time. Horace's boss lived near us, and his wife's brother Bobby lived only two houses away. One day Bobby's wife came to meet me. Her name was Betty Jo, and she had a child a year older than Timmy. His name was Mark and he was considerably bigger than Timmy. Betty Jo often brought Mark over to play with Timmy. Mark was always trying to get Timmy to leave the yard, but he wouldn't cross that imaginary line. Betty Jo would come and make a pot of coffee; then we would just sit and talk. I hadn't had an adult to talk to in a long time. Horace and I never talked.

One day time had just gotten away and I had to rush to fix dinner. Betty Jo said, "Calm down. We'll cook it together." I didn't want Horace to get mad. Things had been going so well. He hadn't lost his temper in a long time. We fixed fried chicken, mashed potatoes, corn, peas, cornbread and iced tea. Bobby came over, and Horace got home at 5:30. He was surprised they were there, but he was okay with it.

Christmas had come and gone and it was summer again. I loved Christmas. We would go in the woods and cut down an awful-looking tree and decorate it. We never had much money, so store-bought Christmas presents were rare. I taught Tim and Regina Christmas songs. My mom had moved to Ruston (a few hours away), so I hardly ever saw her anymore. Horace's boss, Claude, and his wife, Margaret, had a boy a couple of years older than Timmy. He was small like Timmy, but one size bigger. Margaret got her sister-in-law, Betty Jo, to ask me if it would hurt my feelings if she offered me some clothes that Ken had outgrown. I was thankful to her, as we didn't have much money. She gave Timmy some really nice clothes, and I made dresses for Regina, Tracey and myself.

Horace came home one day and said we were moving out to the country. If he would take care of the landlord's horses, we could live there for half the normal rent. The house was very small and needed a lot of fixing up. I didn't want to move so far away, not now, just as I had found someone to talk to, but I didn't want any problems with Horace.

There was so much to do to that house. Horace's sister gave us some leftover paint and wallpaper. Horace didn't help at all. Regina, Timmy and I did all the work. Things were going well, though. Timmy was three, Tracey two. Timmy had a Shetland pony that Horace's sister let him ride. It had belonged to her youngest and was now just the right size for Timmy. He would ride him in the yard all day playing cowboys, Timmy was getting good at riding. Horace kept saying he was going to put him on a big horse soon; that scared me to death. Timmy wasn't a baby anymore; Horace took him places like the cotton gin, where he let Timmy ride on the cotton picker with him.

That July I became pregnant again. I was twenty-two and having my third baby. I loved kids, but never having any money bothered me. Still I learned to make the best of it. I had become very domestic! I learned to cut vines and make wreaths, sew pillows for Christmas gifts, and can foods. I guess I was adjusting to living in a small country town. Horace hadn't really lost his temper in a while. He still yelled a lot, but he hadn't been physical.

On April 7, 1971, Sandra Estelle Smith was born weighing an even seven pounds. I had a very hard delivery with her. I hemorrhaged and had to have a blood transfusion. Sandy had dark brown eyes, dark brown hair and Timmy's complexion. As Tracey had been given my mother's name for her middle name, Sandy was given my mother-in-law's name for her middle name. Mom had come to visit and wanted Regina to come to live with her. I told Regina that it was her decision. Regina said she wanted to try it. I was surely going to miss her help with the kids, but I understood.

Not long after that, Horace's nephew was getting married and we were supposed to go to the rehearsal dinner. Tammy, his thirteen-year-old cousin, had come over to spend the weekend and was helping me. Horace came home in a really bad mood. He was mad at his boss, and they had gotten into an argument. He said he was going to quit. I said, "Horace, what are we going to do? We live from paycheck to paycheck as it is."

"Shut up!" he yelled. "It's none of your damn business!" I did.

Tracey started crying. She didn't want to put on her dress. I was fussing with her and slapped her on the leg and told her to behave. She always misbehaved when her daddy was home. Horace came into the room and told me that since I spanked Tracey, I would have to spank Timmy, too. I said, "That's crazy! Timmy hasn't done anything wrong."

He grabbed Timmy and started hitting him. I tried to take Timmy away from him. Tracey had stopped crying and was running to Timmy. Horace hit me with his fist. He knocked me unconscious this time. When I came to, Tammy had a cold rag on my head, and Timmy was rubbing my face. Horace had left the house. Tammy said, "Betty, look in the mirror!"

I screamed. I had a big knot under my eye already turning blue. We put ice on it and in about an hour the whole side of my face was swollen and turning blue. By this time the knot was black. Tammy wanted me to go to the doctor. I told her I would go if it didn't get better by the morning. I knew the clinic was closed on Saturday, but Tammy didn't. The next morning I looked even worse. I had a neighbor who worked in a doctor's office, and we walked the half mile to her house. When she saw me she immediately wanted to take me to the hospital. I told her no. She said that she could see where the blood vessels had burst in my eye. The knot revealed a cut now, and she said I should keep an ice pack on it. The headache was killing me, so she gave me something for the pain. Not only had I missed the rehearsal, but I didn't go to the wedding either.

That night we were all asleep when Horace came in. He had been at the wedding. He changed clothes and climbed into bed. He didn't bother me. He just went to sleep. About an hour later someone knocked on the door. I didn't move. I had an ice pack on my face. Horace answered the door; it was his mom and his sister Charlotte. They had just come by to see how I was and to see the baby. Horace told them that I had a migraine and not to bother me. They came into the room anyway. I was covered up so they couldn't see my face. They insisted that I get up. When I did, Horace's mother went crazy! She told him off and he went outside.

Tracey, Sandy and Tim

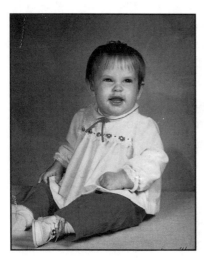

Tracey, Tim and Little Tonya (cousin)

Sandy 3 months

She told me to get my babies—that we were leaving. I told
her I had to stay. I said I had three kids and that was too
much for her to take on. She finally left and Horace returned to the house and lay down on the couch. I turned off
the lights and went back to bed. The next morning I looked
even worse.

The next week he was still mad at his boss. He came
home late one evening, and I was really scared. I was pray-
ing he wouldn't come home drunk or mad. I just couldn't
take it again. When he got home he told me we were moving to Jigger, a small town close to Winnsboro, where my
grandparents lived. I knew Tim would be upset, because the
move would mean returning the pony that Horace's sister
was letting him ride. Horace said he had gotten a job driving a truck. He told me that if he trained this man's horses
in his spare time, we wouldn't have to pay any rent, plus he
was going to make $150 per week. He then said we would
go see the house the next day.

The next day we went to see the house. It was awful. It
was in the middle of nowhere about a mile away from town.
Town was a general store, gas station/post office combina-
tion and two churches. The house was an old barn. It still
had hay in it, but Horace was quick to point out that at one
time it had been a house because it had plumbing in it.

Trying to make that house livable was a lot of work.
Horace's new boss had three sons who helped me clean it
out. Since the truck we had been driving belonged to
Horace's old boss, we had to get a car. We found an old station wagon to buy. It was a good thing we didn't have to
pay rent, or we couldn't have afforded the car.

I worked very hard painting, hanging wallpaper and fixing up the house. I had to use old paint that his boss had, so
the colors weren't too good, but it was clean. Horace was

gone three days at a time hauling cotton and vegetables. He would be home one night and then gone again. We started going to the two churches, alternating weeks. One church was the Church of Christ and the other was Pentecostal. It was surely different from what I had been used to. I was Catholic and the last church we had gone to was Baptist. The kids liked the Pentecostal church. Kids didn't have to sit still there, and they loved the singing. Timmy, Tracey and Joey, a neighbor's son, would sing trios occasionally in the church. Timmy loved it. They all wanted to hold the mic. They were so cute. We went to a baptism one Sunday afternoon at the river. Timmy watched what happened and told the preacher that he wanted to be baptized, too. The preacher and I agreed that he was too young for that.

One afternoon, I had just put the kids down for a nap after lunch when Horace's boss came to the door and said there had been an accident and Horace had been taken to the burn unit at Baton Rouge General Hospital. I gathered up the kids and called Tammy to go with me. Mr. Fawler, Horace's boss, gave me $150 dollars for gas and expenses. We loaded up the car and left. I had no idea where the hospital was, but I found it. Horace had received third-degree burns over 25 percent of his upper body. He had been hauling phone posts and fueling the truck when somehow a fire broke out. The gas hose sprayed him. He was in really bad shape. His mom and sister came to the hospital. Tammy's mother, Aunt Margaret, picked up my kids to keep them for me.

After a couple of days we had to move Horace to the Charity Hospital in Monroe since we didn't have any insurance. He was there three months. All his truck-driving buddies would chip in each week and help us out. I stayed at the hospital all the time. One night a week I would leave and stay all night with my kids. My uncle or Horace's brothers-in-law would relieve me so that I could go home and be with the kids. Aunt Margaret and Mom would watch the kids for me. Needless to say, we lost my car because I could no longer afford the payments. I wanted to get a job, but Horace refused. His boss gave him seventy-five dollars per week as a disability payment, and we had to get food stamps. I hated that but could do nothing more.

When Horace was released from the hospital, he went to work driving a truck for a different company, so we moved again. This was our seventh move! This time we moved into a small house. One of Horace's friends had an old car and said we could have it if we paid off the rest of what he owed, which was $110 per month for the $1200 he owed on it. Things got better. I learned to love the country. A few years passed without Horace losing his temper. I think being on the road helped, because when he came home, he seemed to have missed us. He started teaching Timmy to ride big horses. Timmy loved it.

Betty in 1969

Tim and Santa in 1971

One of the many houses they lived in before
Horace and Betty divorced

Ranch where Horace
taught Tim to ride

Sandy, 2; Tracy, 4; Tim, 5

Chapter 9

When Timmy was old enough to start kindergarten, I went to the school board office to register him. I gave the clerk his birth certificate and shot record and explained that even though his birth certificate said McGraw, I wanted him registered as Smith. Timmy was too young to know his stepdad was not his real dad. He had never seen, nor heard, from Tug. The clerk said that she could not do that. I begged her, but she said I would have to get a lawyer. My grandparents knew a lawyer who was running for district attorney. I met with him and told him my problem. He charged me $125. It was hard coming up with the money, but he let me pay in installments. I budgeted my money and paid him twenty dollars each payday. We met with the judge, who ruled that since Tug had never given any support to the child, we could temporarily change his name to Smith in the best interest of the child. This would not be an adoption and would stand until he was 18 years of age. He could then choose his own name. He was enrolled in school a few days late.

Timmy loved school, but Tracey really missed him. She couldn't understand why she couldn't go. The only kids who lived nearby were school age, so she had no playmates. Sandy was too young; she was only two. It took a while for me to let Timmy ride the bus. I just couldn't put my baby on the bus. But he wanted to ride and the boy next door was eight and said he would watch out for him.

Horace's job was going well. We still didn't have much money, but we were able to pay our bills. Horace still had a bad temper but he hadn't lost control and hit me for a long time. He screamed and yelled a lot and scared the kids and me, but he wasn't as violent as in the past. A couple of times, when he was working on the car or something else and broke something or hit his hand, he threw things, cursed and yelled. I was just glad he wasn't hitting me or my kids. I hoped that maybe he was learning not to take things out on us.

Horace was on the road quite a bit that year. My mom had moved back to Florida and remarried. That Christmas I decided to fix a big spaghetti dinner and invite relatives over. I was able to see my grandmother pretty often, since we had gotten a car and she lived only 15 minutes away. Horace agreed to the dinner, and I made gifts for every-body—little sachets with dried wild flowers in them and boxes of homemade candy. I loved making candy and cook-ies at Christmas. We had a fabulous time. I think those two-and-a-half years were the happiest Horace and I had togeth-er.

Then March came around. Horace came home one eve-ning and said, "Guess who I ran into today?"

"Who?" I asked.

"Claude!"

"How is he?" I asked.

"He's fine. He lost his foreman and wanted to know if I was interested."

I just stood there for a minute and said, "I thought you liked your job here, being on the road. You like that and we've been getting along great. We're happy here. Why would you want to change?"

"Well, Claude said he would give us a house, a truck

and pay me what I'm making now. I'll be the boss. I want to do this, Betty."

"But, Horace, I like it here."

He got very angry. "I'm the one who's going to make the decision! We will move again!"

Again, I had to fix up another house, but it wasn't too bad. The only bathroom was on the back porch. It consisted of a shower stall, toilet and sink. It was an old house. We eventually put a full bathroom in the house and got it all painted and spruced up. It had a lot of pretty flowers in the yard, and I loved that. I enrolled Timmy and Tracey in school.

Every now and then I was able to save a couple of dollars, and after a while I had enough to buy a new couch. The one I had was an old one that my mother had given to me, and it had become a rag. I was able to buy a fake leather couch and chair. I hadn't had anything in so long that I had forgotten what it was like. I also bought material and made the girls matching dresses; Timmy got a new pair of pants and shoes, and I made him a couple of shirts. We lived in that house longer than any other throughout our marriage. We moved ten times in the eight-and-a-half years we were married.

Timmy was in the second grade now and Tracey was in the first. Sandy was three and quite the pistol. She had tea parties and played dolls all day long. She was so different from Tracey, who wouldn't play with dolls. She liked stuffed animals and didn't like "sissy" stuff. Sandy loved playing house. She called me Miss Betty when she was playing. She would pretend she was a neighbor coming to visit. She had a very vivid imagination. She made up stories about anything and everything.

The trashmen came every Friday. They would come into

Tim, Tracey, Sandy and
cousins Jon and
Stephan

Tracey, Sandy, their
grandfather, and
Tim in 1974

Tim's eighth birthday

the backyard, take the cans around front to empty them and then return them to the backyard. Sandy always sat on the back door step and said hi and talked to them. They would wave back at her. One evening, Horace drove in and Sandy went to meet him. He started cursing, "Those damn %$#@*&! They'd better start putting the trash cans up." The men had left the cans in the front. The next Friday Sandy was sitting on the steps waiting as usual to say hi. When the trashmen got the cans she said, "My daddy said you damn %$#@*&! better put those trash cans back this time!" The men were dying laughing at her. I made her come inside and explained that little girls do not talk like that.

Horace was working long days and was really tired when he got home. So he wasn't always in a good mood. I tried hard to keep the kids out of his hair and to keep things peaceful. I continued to have dinner ready for him as soon as he got home. Horace started riding horses with his buddies again; Timmy went some of the time and could ride really well.

Whenever anything broke in the house, I tried everything I could to fix it because I didn't like asking Horace to fix anything. He would always get mad because he was tired and would start throwing things. So I always tried to get someone else to fix things. I often called Billie, and she would send Dee over to help me. Horace didn't like me being friendly with Billie because she was an independent woman and bossy, and he didn't like women to be like that. Whenever he yelled at me when Billie was around, she would tell him to quit talking to me that way. And if he told me to get him something like a beer, she would tell him to get off his ass and get it himself.

One evening Timmy was going to be in a school recital

and Horace was home. Timmy had to beg Horace to go. Timmy was the announcer and sang "The Battle Hymn of the Republic." He was terrific; no one could believe how well he sang. I told everyone that you have to love to sing to sing well, and Timmy loved to sing. Timmy was very shy until he got on stage, but once there, he would loosen up. Afterward, he was embarrassed at everyone fussing over him.

Horace was working for his old boss Claude, again. Margaret started bringing Timmy clothes again, which really helped out. The little league was starting up, and Timmy would be old enough to play. In a box of clothes that Margaret gave him were a pair of cleats. He was so excited. I saved money and was able to buy him a glove and ball. He tried to get Horace to play ball with him, but he wouldn't, so I started teaching Timmy how to play baseball. I still felt like I did when he was in my belly—I wanted him to be somebody, maybe be terrific at baseball so someday his real dad, Tug, would have to sit up and take notice. The only sport Horace was interested in was horseback riding. He started going riding every weekend with his old buddies. He also started having his "mad spells" again and being mean to the kids. I tried to keep them out of his hair. Occasionally he would take Timmy to ride horses, which scared me. I was afraid that Timmy would do something to upset Horace. Each Sunday after riding, I would cook for all of Horace's buddies. I liked to cook and enjoyed entertaining. Everyone always bragged on my cooking. (Even if I say so myself, I am a very good cook.)

Things were going okay, and sometimes the girls and I would watch them ride horses. I didn't know how to ride, but Timmy was doing great and Tracey was starting on the ponies. It was hard watching the kids and trying to keep them away from the horses and cows. Horace was always so jealous if one of the guys riding horses with him even spoke to me. He would go crazy. It was easier to stay away and keep down the potential trouble. Even after all the problems with Horace, I do thank him for one thing. No matter what his reasons for not letting me work, I believe that staying home helped me build the closeness I share with my children.

My mother was living back in Jacksonville, Florida, and wanted us to visit. I really wanted to go, but Horace didn't. I hadn't seen Mary in so long, and I wanted to go home. It took some doing for me to convince Horace to go, but he finally agreed when Mom sent us the money for the trip. We could go for five days. I could hardly wait. I hadn't seen the ocean in so long. We traveled at night so the kids would sleep most of the way.

As soon as I got to Mom's, I called Mary. Mary had gotten married and had two sons. Her oldest was a year older than my youngest. She had married one of the boys in the band we knew. I had sung with them on a few occasions in the teen clubs. I couldn't believed she married Mike Reeves. I teased her about it because she had hated him in the beginning. He followed her around like a puppy. She used to call him a pest, and now they were married!

Mary and I had a good visit. Horace wouldn't leave us alone though. Mike asked Horace if he wanted to ride and get a beer with him. Even though Horace didn't realize it, Mike knew "the girls" wanted to be alone, and he thought this would be the only way we could spend time together. Mary kept looking at me oddly throughout the visit. When the guys left, she said, "Betty, you've changed. Really changed. What's going on with you."

"Nothing," I responded.

"Betty, I know you, what's going on in your life that has changed you so? What happened to your spirit? It's gone!"

She kept quizzing me. I wanted so much to tell her how unhappy I was and how fearful I was, but I was so ashamed. I wanted to bare my soul, but how could I tell anyone what my life was really like? Even Mary. Somehow though, she knew. We had always been so connected to each other. Horace couldn't wait to leave, so we had to cut our visit short by two days. I didn't want to return, but had no choice.

Mary and I wrote when we could, and I heard from my mom pretty often, but since they both worked, it wasn't as often as I would have liked. Timmy and Tracey were in school, so it was just Sandy and I at home. Horace still hadn't lost his temper like before. We had a few arguments from time to time, usually because someone spoke to me when we were in town. It didn't matter who it was—an old friend, a stranger. Horace had become jealous of everyone, particularly if they were my age, even his friends. When I took the kids to watch Horace ride horses, and his younger friends said hello, Horace would go nuts and make me go home. The kids and I stopped going so I could minimize trouble.

Mom had called Horace's boss and left word for me to call her in Florida (we still couldn't afford a phone). When I called her, she told me she was going to marry Herbert Doctors. We had known him and his wife when I was younger. I use to babysit for his five daughters occasionally. He and his wife had been divorced for a long time. He and my mom had run into each other and had been dating for quite a while. I was happy for my mom because Herb is a great man.

The next year my grandmother became ill. Mom came to

Louisiana and stayed with her until her death. Soon, my Mom and Herb moved to Monroe, Louisiana, where mom opened a beauty shop. Mom and Horace's sister talked me into going to beauty school. Sandy would be in school soon, and I would be able to work. Of course, Horace said we couldn't afford for me to go to school. That was just his attempt to keep me at home. But I went to the vocational rehabilitation office, and they agreed to pay for me to go to school!

Horace really didn't like me going to school. Dinner would not be ready at the mandatory time of 5:15 p.m. He kept trying to force me to quit. We got into a big argument one night and he hit me. For the first time in a long time, the kids were scared. They told me, "Mom, we don't like Daddy hitting you anymore." Horace left as usual, and I talked to the kids. I didn't want them hating their father, so I told them that he really didn't mean to hit me, that he just got real tired sometimes and that made him get angry very easily. To keep peace, I reduced the schedule at the beauty school to part time. The rehab money was cut off as a result, but Mom said she would pay for it if I would finish school.

Easter

Tracey, Connie (cousin), Sandy and Tim

Chapter 10

After I had been in school six months, I went to the clinic
for my regular checkup and to get my birth control pills.
Two days later, the clinic sent me a letter telling me to return, as something was wrong with the tests. They made an
appointment for me with a gynecologist in Monroe. The
tests he needed to do cost $80. Horace was mad that it cost
so much money and said there was nothing wrong with me.
I had to go back for a biopsy, which would cost another
$50. I was so frightened and worried about what was wrong
with me that I didn't want to have to listen to Horace yell at
me about the money, so I didn't show him the second bill. I
figured I could sew for some friends and make the money to
pay the doctor. I had to wait three more days for the results.

When I found out I needed a biopsy, it was like someone
hit me in the stomach. I sat there telling myself, "Betty it
happens all the time. It's just a test to be sure. It'll be fine."
I got my mom to go with me and told her and no one else.
Tracey and Timmy were in school, and Sandy was with us.
She was only four and a half. They did my biopsy on a Friday and said they'd call on Monday evening with results.
Actually they didn't call until Tuesday. We had no phone, so
they called a neighbor who came and got me to the phone.
The nurse naturally made sure it was me and said I needed
to come in Wednesday and see the doctor. I knew something
was wrong. I told no one.

Fixing dinner that night, I was in a fog. My mind was just wandering. I truly don't remember what went through it. I went on and did everything as usual and no one said anything or even noticed, but no one was around but my kids and Horace when he got home from work. The next morning, the kids went to school, and I went to the doctor. When they called me in, I asked the nurse to watch Sandy because I didn't want her in there. The doctor told me my test showed a malignancy. I had cancer, and I needed surgery. It was a tumor and it was the type that is sometimes recurring. They wouldn't know how far along or what stage it was in until they did surgery. He then suggested I get a second opinion. He also asked if I wanted more children. I said I had wanted one more later. He told me I could get pregnant and postpone surgery for nine months. "No," I said, "if it's cancer, let's do it now. God has blessed me with three healthy children, so we'll do it now!

Cancer in the '60s and '70s was still a scary subject. It was known as the "C" word. People were still scared of it and treated people differently if they knew they had it. That's probably one of the reasons I didn't say much about it until it was over with. I didn't want the kids to be scared, but I also didn't want them going to school and talking about it and have people treating them differently.

Cancer is scary. Mary's husband, Mike, died of cancer just three years ago. He was younger than Mary and I; he was only 41 at the time. His cancer was in the latter stages when they found it, so after they found it and did surgery, he didn't last long. They found it in November, and he died the following June. This left Mary a widow at age 43 with four teenage boys to take care of. It can strike anyone at anytime. Check-ups are important. If you can't afford a doctor on your own, there are free clinics. My cancer was found in a free clinic. Cancer doesn't always have to kill anyone. Early detection is the key.

I paid my bill and left with Sandy. She naturally chattered all the way home in the car about how she now was going to be a nurse. She said, "Mommy, are you still sick?"

"Yes, a little," I said.

"Well, I'll take care of you 'cause I'm a nurse." My eyes swelling with tears, I went to my mother's (she was working at a convenience store as a manager) and told her what the doctor said.

"That's nonsense," she said. "You're only 27. You're too young for all this."

I didn't tell my kids when it happened. All they knew was Mommy was sick and had to stay in the hospital for a while. I didn't let them see me emotional about it.

Afterward and when they were older, I had conversations with each one individually about it. It was traumatic but I'm good at handling things. Each time a crisis comes up, I deal with it in my own philosophical way. The one thing I've always had with my kids is communication. It's hard when I know they have a problem and they don't open up, but I understand. I think they learned from me when they were younger, because they talked about everything. They still talk to me more than most children do to their parents, at least more than the kids I know. But as the years go by, they get more and more independent and that's what is supposed to happen. I was independent early because of a have-to situation, so I learned to handle things on my own.

I had always been the strong person everyone went to with problems, but who could I talk to? I wished that I was back in Florida and on the beach where I could walk and think. It always helped before. . . . I went home and I called the new doctor in town, Dr. Johnson. He was young and just

setting up practice as a surgeon. I made an appointment, and
my mom went with me to help with Sandy. The second
opinion was the same. I saw him on Friday and he scheduled surgery for Monday. He and his staff were wonderful. I
explained I had no insurance. He said I'd have to give the
hospital $500 and I could pay him a little at a time. I am
very grateful to him. He made me feel confident because he
didn't even doubt that he could get it all. He said he'd do
the surgery, do another biopsy and check it, and then we'd
go from there. So I went home. Mom said she'd keep Timmy, but I knew she couldn't handle all three of them. I
asked Horace's Aunt Margaret to keep the girls, and she
said she would. I told Horace, and all he said was "What
will this cost?" I just looked at him and went into the kitch-
en. Finally that night, he asked me if I was scared. I said
no, that Dr. Johnson said he could get all of it.

I think I was fine until Sunday. All day I was nervous. I
tried not to think about it, but actually it was all I thought
about. I didn't sleep at all; I was up and down all night. I'd
go look at the kids or just sit in a chair looking out the window. Horace got up, dressed for work, kissed me on the
cheek and said he'd come up to the hospital after work. I
got the kids ready for school. Aunt Margaret came to pick
up Sandy. She said she would pick Tracey up after school
and Mom would pick up Timmy. The doctor said I'd only
have to stay five days. This was about two weeks before
Easter. The kids would be out of school for Easter vacation
the next week. Mom had given me the $500 for the hospital.
She knew Horace and I didn't have it. I drove myself to the
hospital.

I had to pay the hospital before they checked me in and
did all my blood work. I felt odd being in the hospital, because I felt fine. I wasn't sick; I never had any pain. The

Tim, 5th grade

Tracey, Horace, Sandy, Betty and Tim

cancer was found because of my pap smear. I went to the
free clinic every six months for birth control pills, and they
always did a pap smear and checkup before giving me the
refill. I thanked God for the fact that I always got my check-
ups and hoped it meant we got this cancer early enough. Dr.
Johnson came in to talk to me; he had a way of making me
feel comfortable and confident. My mom came over after
work and said she'd be there in the morning when I went to
surgery. Horace, Aunt Margaret and Horace's sister Barbara
came to the hospital. Barbara asked if I needed her to do
anything. I said no, just pray.

My mom and my friend Billy were there bright and early
since I was supposed to go to surgery at 7 a.m., Horace
came before he went to work and said he'd go on to work
since Mom and Billy were there. I agreed there was no reason for everyone to sit around. Billy and I had been friends
for a while. She had three kids also, and I was really glad
she was there.

When I came to, I was in my room and Dr. Johnson was
holding my hand. He said everything was terrific, that the
tumor had no spurs; it was like a golf ball. He did radiation
around the area, but said the tests would be back in the
morning, although he was 99 percent sure he got it all. It
was that 1 percent that scared me, but I acted confident. I
guess my Mom and Billy called everybody, because my
room was full with family and friends that night. Even the
priest from the Catholic church where Billy went to church
was there. I was Catholic, but I had been going to the Baptist church with the kids. I did get some flowers to cheer me
up: a big vase of roses from my mom. But Horace didn't
think of anything like that.

The next morning Dr. Johnson came in and said they had
gotten all of the cancer and I could probably go home in

about three days. Everyone was gone now, and I was by myself. I could breathe—the tests were good. I had a good cry; this crisis was over.

Being in the hospital gave me time to do some serious thinking. I'd been so busy taking care of kids that I never had the time to just look at my life and ask, what if? What would my children do if something happened to me? I wouldn't want Horace to raise them; they needed me. I realized I was unhappy. I was scared all the time. The kids were nervous wrecks. Tracey was withdrawn. Tim's nerves were shot. He shook all the time. Sandy always had a bellyache. I knew her problems were nerves, also. Sure, there were good days. Being married to Horace wasn't all bad; but those bad days were getting harder to tolerate.

I think I felt I was not a good enough person inside. I felt like I was beneath everyone else. I had gotten pregnant as a teen, the father of my child had turned his back on me and I hadn't finished high school. All that made me less of a person. I had lost all my self-confidence. But this cancer scare made me wake up. I realized I was somebody, I was smart and talented. I could go to school, I could work, I could get out on my own and take control of my life and my children's lives. I knew I could do it. I knew I was going to do it. I just didn't know when. But I knew I wanted to get out. I was ready to get my self-respect back.

A lot of women get in the situation I was in. We lose all self-respect and we hang on because of the kids . . . thinking, hoping things will change and get better—they never do. When a relationship becomes physically violent, GET OUT OF THERE. Life's too short. But abuse is not just physical. NO PERSON should have to put up with any type of abuse, physical or verbal. Hold your head up, take control of your life and go forward.

The day after surgery, I began running a high fever and my stomach swelled. I had developed an infection. I ended up staying two weeks in the hospital. They had to give me IV antibiotics. Dr. Johnson reopened my wound so it could heal from the inside out. The nurses had to clean it every-day with peroxide and betadine solutions. It was really pain-ful!

I finally convinced the doctor that I could recuperate at home and quite frankly could not afford to stay in the hospital. He agreed to let me go home as long as someone was there to take care of me and I stayed in bed. Aunt Margaret and Tammy said they would help me. Horace's boss hired a lady to help me with the housework and cooking for one week after I went home. Aunt Margret became my nurse, changing and cleaning my wound. I finally got my strength back and started putting on some weight.

Betty, Tim, Sandy and Tracey

Chapter 11

About six weeks after my surgery Elvis came to Monroe on a U.S. tour. Horace's Aunt Margaret bought me two tickets so I could take Timmy. It was his birthday present. He was a real big Elvis fan. We both were. We were going with her kids, Tammy, Tom and Kathy. The night before the concert Timmy came down with the mumps. He was running a high fever, and the doctor said I shouldn't take him out. He sure was disappointed. We brought him back an Elvis shirt and record. I think he'll always remember that birthday since he never had a chance to see Elvis again. He died the next year.

Several months after my surgery, at the end of the school year, Timmy's music teacher stopped by the house on Sunday afternoon and told us that the little theater in town was putting on a production of "The Music Man." She wanted Timmy to audition for the leading part of Winthrop Parooh. I told her that I didn't want Timmy to get his hopes up and then be disappointed. She said, "I think he'll get the part. He's so talented and has such a beautiful voice." She told me she would work up a song with him and that the audition would be the following Sunday. I finally agreed.

I told Horace about the visit; he didn't like it one bit. He said it was nonsense, but we went anyway. Timmy was one of six boys auditioning for the lead. He was the first one they listened to that day. He sang "The Battle Hymn of the

Republic." When he got to the second line, the director turned to me and handed me a copy of the script. When Timmy was finished, everyone stood up and applauded. Timmy walked over to the director. The director said, "Timmy, do you think you can learn to talk with a lisp?" Timmy just shrugged his shoulders. The director then said, "Son, when a director asks you if you can do something, you just say, 'Yes, sir' and go home and learn it." We all laughed. He told the other boys they could have walk-on parts and that rehearsals would start next week.

The girls and I went to rehearsals with Timmy. They started at 5:30 p.m. Horace had been coming home at 6:30 p.m., and when we got home, he was always mad because his dinner wasn't ready and I wasn't there. I just ignored him. He never wanted us to do anything except stay home.

One evening I dropped Timmy off, and the girls and I went back home. When it came time to pick Timmy up, Horace told me I couldn't go get him. He said he could walk home. I told him he was crazy. It was 9 p.m. and Timmy was only nine years old. Horace took the keys away from me and left. The girls and I walked to get Timmy. We were almost thirty minutes late. You could tell by Timmy's expression that he probably realized Horace was acting up. The kids were used to it. Timmy didn't say anything.

I apologized to the director, saying I had car problems and had to walk. He offered to take us home, and I gladly excepted. By the time we got home, Horace was really mad. He told Timmy he would have to quit the play. I told him he couldn't do that to Timmy or the people who where putting on the play. We got into a big argument. He started hitting me, and the kids jumped on him, trying to make him stop. I got the kids into their room and locked the door. I slept with them in their room.

Tim in *The Music Man*

Timmy said, "Mom, what are we going to do? Do I have to quit the play?"

I told him, "No baby, you'll do the play; they are all depending on you. You want to, don't you?"

"Sure, Mom. Yes, I do."

"Well, Horace will get over it," I assured my son. "You'll do the play. I promise!" The play ran for one week and Timmy did a great job! I was indeed proud of him.

At that point I was finally beginning to wake up. I was only 27 years old. I had gone through too many adversities. Now it was time to pick up my life and my children's lives. They deserved better and I deserved better. I was different after my surgery. I had changed. I was not a little beat-down girl anymore. I had finally grown up and become a woman. I knew I was getting out; I just didn't know when yet. I had had enough! I had lived through too much. I had even had cancer and survived. Now it was time to take control of my life. I could go to work and take care of myself and my kids if I had to. But once again, I stayed.

I can't remember why, but a few months later Horace was on the rampage again. This time he picked up a chair to hit me. I put my hand up to block the blow and he broke my thumb. I went crazy! I dove into him with a Coke bottle and hit him over and over again on the head. I just kept hitting him. I couldn't stop. He fell to the floor screaming for me to stop. I did. Then I got really angry. Not at Horace, but at myself. I had been scared to death of this man for over eight years, and the very first time I fight back, I find out that he's afraid of me. All one hundred and five pounds of me. I put the kids in the car and left, never looking back.

Finally leaving gave me my Independence Day! This was it. Betty Dagostino was finally back. Look out, world. I can do this. I can get on with my life—push forward and make life better and more fulfilling for me and my children. I've always had three great children. I thank God every day for each of them. They were my rock through all of this. When Horace and I divorced, Timmy was nine years old, Tracy was eight and Sandy was six. It was hard on all of us, but we pulled together. They had to work as hard as I did. They had always been with me and now they had to stay with babysitters and adjust to not having me all the time. But it was better than living in fear.

I went to my girlfriend Billie's house. Billie's husband and Horace had worked together. She took me to the hospital to have my thumb fixed. I stayed with her for a few days, then went to see my Mom. I asked if the kids and I could stay with them until we could get a place of our own. She agreed, wondering why it had taken me so long to leave in the first place.

The next week, I went to see an attorney and filed for a divorce. I got a job as a waitress at a restaurant. Horace would call my mom's cursing; I wouldn't talk to him. He would find the car and either flatten my tires or pull wires from the engine. I had to get a restraining order against him. Since my mom had helped us get the car I was driving, I told Horace that I would keep the car and he could have all the furniture. All I wanted, other than out, was the children's clothing. I was able to get his cousin to go and get the clothes for me.

One afternoon Horace called and told me to come get the rest of my personal stuff. I got Tammy to go with me. When we got there, all my stuff—photo albums with pictures of me when I was a teenage dancer, baby pictures of the children, record albums—was piled in the front yard.

Horace had soaked them with gasoline. As I drove up, he set fire to it all. I did manage to grab a few things out of the fire before he headed at me. Tammy and I got in the car and left. Most all of my things were gone, but I still had my freedom. (The pictures in this book were all I had left, and even some of those had to be collected from relatives.)

Tim 8th grade

Chapter 12

I decided to make a permanent home for my children. I talked to my girlfriend Betty Jo. She said when she got divorced, she had been able to get a Farmer's Home loan. She said it was easy to get if you had a low income, which I certainly did. A builder gave me an application, and before my divorce was final I was approved for the $21,000 loan. The hard part was getting Horace to sign a document stating that he had nothing to do with my loan. He did anything he could to try to make things difficult. It took my attorney a long time, but he was able to pressure him into signing. It was nearly six months before we were able to take possession of the house.

The house was a brick three-bedroom with one and a half baths. It had central heat with no air conditioning, but we had never had anything this nice! My mortgage payments were $110 per month for the first year, which was great because Horace was to pay $200 per month in child support. Needless to say, it was a long time before I ever saw any money, and then it was sporadic at best. I could not depend on that income at all. I had to work two waitress jobs to make ends meet. Horace remained hostile for a long time. I did let him see the kids when he wanted, if they wanted to go.

I had two twin-size beds, a full-size mattress and a television when we moved into our new home. I had to buy a refrigerator, washer and dryer on time. Dishwashers and things of that type were not even dreamed of. Slowly, we furnished the house. The one-acre lot I had chosen was a wooded one with a small lake behind it. The lake had an island in the middle of it right behind our house. I used the lake as a substitute for the beach back home. I could sit out there and think. I built a dock, which became my quiet place when I needed to think. I had thought of moving back to Florida when Horace and I finally divorced, but my kids loved their dad and I couldn't take them that far away. No matter what our problems, Horace needed the children and I knew he loved them. After all, he was the only father figure they had.

The lake and island were always tempting to the kids. I recall one day when Timmy, Tracey and Sandy called me at work to ask if they could camp out on the island. I said, "Yes, but make sure the back porch light is on and you take a flashlight." I had to work a little later until the hostess for the night shift could get to work. By the time I got home, it was getting dark but I could see that they already had the tents set up. When I opened the door the lights were on, so I called, "I'm home." No answer. I went into the kitchen and fixed myself a Coke. I looked out back. I knew Timmy was on the island with his friends. I could hear music and see lights on the island, which was odd since there was no electricity there. I looked around and saw plugged into the back porch an extension cord . . . one of those big orange ones. I got my flashlight and went to investigate. The cord ran across the yard, up to our dock and across the water where another cord was plugged into it. They had attached a board to the end of the dock and bent a nail in an attempt to hold it up out of the water. I started screaming toward the lake. The kids finally heard me and turned off the music. I yelled for them to come back across to the house. Timmy, Tracey and her friend rowed across the lake to me in our small aluminum boat. I asked, "Who all is out there? And, where is Sandy?"

"She's at the babysitter's house," Timmy said.

I went back across the lake in the boat with Timmy. His friend Lance was still out there. They had taken Timmy's TV, radio, fan and lamps from his room. They also had a grill on which they were cooking steaks from our freezer. The only thing missing was room service. I explained to them how dangerous it was to string those extension cords across the lake and reminded them that water and electricity don't mix.

"Guys, camping means camping!" I said. "None of these conveniences." I unplugged everything. I had Timmy row me back to the house and left them with flashlights only. The next morning, they rowed their stuff all back to the house.

Money was still tight. I did crafts, like flower arrangements and wreaths, for people to earn extra money. I never had the opportunity to go back to beauty school during my marriage. I decided that I would rather go to night school two nights a week and get my high school diploma. After receiving my diploma, I started business school to learn bookkeeping, so I could get one better paying job and stop working two and three jobs, some at night. I was making more money than before, but I didn't like being gone in the evening.

Finally, after a year, I got a job as a bookkeeper. I had no experience, but they gave me a chance. I worked with a CPA, and he helped me a lot. I was making about $200 a week, so after a while, I quit my night waitress job. I still did flowers. I was able to do a few weddings, and that helped. I was paying my full house payment of $198 on my own with no government help, which made me feel great. The kids were on the free lunch program at school. We were getting by; we were happy.

We lived on a "family" budget. Timmy came home one day and asked if he could get off the free lunch program. He told me it really embarrassed him. So I called for one of our family meetings and talked to all the kids about the free lunch program. It didn't bother the girls, only Timmy. So, as a group, we decided we could afford lunch now, if we watched our money. While we were on the subject of money, Timmy brought up the fact that he needed new jeans.

"Mom," he said, "I realize that we don't have a lot of money, but you get made fun of if you don't wear Levi's or Wranglers. They don't make fun of girls. They can wear anything, but guys need cool clothes or they're nerds."

I just said, "I can't believe this. Things have changed since I was a girl. Nobody cared about labels and brand, especially in jeans." Then I remembered Gant shirts with the loop on the back being the in thing along with socks the same color as your shirt. So I could understand.

The girls agreed. "Mom, he's right. And he needs Reeboks—every boy wears Reeboks."

"Well," I said, "how do you think we can solve the problem?" Timmy said to keep his allowance and save it, Tracey said she'd give Timmy some of her allowance and Sandy said, "He ain't getting none of my allowance." So we came to an agreement to get Timmy jeans and tennis shoes and to stop the free lunch program.

Timmy mowed yards a couple of weekends, and at the end of the month I surprised him with a pair of Wranglers, a pair of Levi's and also a pair of Reeboks. I also got both of the girls a new outfit and shoes. You would have thought Christmas had come early. They all went crazy. Tracy said, "Well, Timmy, now you're a cool dude!"

Sandy, Tracey and Tim

Our back yard in Start

Chapter 13

I was really catching on at my new job, and I enjoyed working there. My babysitter, Cathy, watched the kids after school until I got home at 5 p.m. Timmy was 11, Tracey 10 and Sandy 8. Then came the afternoon I received that dreaded call, the day Timmy found his birth certificate. (See *Preface*) Timmy wanted me to come home. I couldn't believe this was happening. I was hoping to deal with this later. Now how would I tell Timmy this whole story?

I looked over at him sitting beside me in the car. He was holding Tug's baseball cards. He said, "Mom, what kind of a person is Tug McGraw? Do you think he'd like me, if I ever met him?"

"He sure would. He'd be proud of you just like I am."

"Mom?"

"Yes, Tim . . ."

"I sure wish I could meet him."

I couldn't say anything. I just looked straight ahead hoping he couldn't see my tears.

Timmy and I went to the Sonic, grabbed a couple of chili dogs and rode around and talked. Telling him the story of Tug and me didn't take long, because we only knew each other a couple of months. There wasn't much to tell, but I did try and explain how it had happened. I didn't want to place any blame on me or Tug. It had just happened. Timmy was only 11, so it was hard to tell if he understood totally, but he seemed to be accepting it. But, he did want to meet his father. Timmy said, "All this makes little things make more sense now." He had always felt that Horace treated him a little differently from the girls, after the divorce especially. He had thought maybe he was just harder on him because he was a boy, but now it all made sense.

I was always thankful that Horace had never brought Tug up to Timmy. As mean as he was to me, that showed me he did love Timmy because that really could have hurt him. The only times he ever said anything about Tug were when only he and I were present. I'd threaten to leave him if he didn't stop hitting me, and he'd say "Sure, and where are you gonna go? You can't take care of three kids by yourself and nobody wants you. Tug McGraw didn't want you and your kid." That would be worse than a punch or a slap in the face. I'd just withdraw and shut up, thinking he was right. I felt I was not good enough for a long, long time. Until that day I woke up after my surgery and took my life back.

Timmy was excited, as I guess most boys would be. (My real dad is a major league baseball player and famous too.)

"Timmy, now don't just run out telling everyone," I said. "They won't believe you. You've been Timmy Smith for almost 11 years now." I was wasting my breath. One day the girls came home from school and told me that Timmy had been getting into fights. A few days later, the school called me at work; something had happened in one of Timmy's classes. The teacher was talking about truths, and she used as an example Timmy's telling everyone that Tug McGraw was his father. Timmy took it the wrong way, and the kids in class laughed. Timmy ran away from school. He had never been any trouble to anyone, but I guess his emotions were all mixed up. I left work and went home first, hoping to find Timmy. Half the school was in my yard, including the principal, trying to get Timmy to come out of the house. I went in the back door and found Timmy on his bed. He was upset because no one would believe him. I invited the principal to come in. He apologized to Timmy when I handed him Timmy's birth certificate. He said he would share it with Timmy's classmates and get it all straightened out.

After the principal left, Timmy said, "Mom, I need to meet my father. I don't care if he wants to see me or not. I need to see him."

The next day at work, I sat alone in my office. It was obvious that something was bothering me. I'm a talker, so when I'm quiet people start wondering what is wrong. Shirly Lee was one of my best friends, so she knew me pretty well. (I've been blessed to have two best friends in my life, Mary and Shirly. We all still keep in touch.) She came in and brought me a cup of tea.

"Okay, girl," she said. "What's wrong?" I told her about Timmy and Tug. Nobody but a few family members knew this. Another good friend, Cathy, came in while we were talking. Shirly said to Cathy, "Girl, you need to sit down and hear this."

I told them the whole story. "And now Timmy wants to meet his real father and I'm scared to death!" I said. "He's wealthy and famous. What boy wouldn't want a baseball player for his dad? What if they meet and Tug wants him? He's a wonderful kid. He just might!"

"Listen, you're a great mom," Shirly said. "Timmy loves you and he knows who loves him. You won't lose him!!"

I always wanted Timmy to know his dad. That's why I wouldn't let Horace adopt him. He had a right to know the truth someday; I just wasn't prepared. So, after a good cry with my friends, I called Philadelphia. I left word for Tug to call me, that it was personal and very important. The following day, a man called me screening my call to Tug. I told him the matter was personal. He then asked me if it was an emergency and I told him no, but it was very, very important. Two days later the phone rang in my office. Tug was on the other end. Every muscle in my body went limp. I had not spoken to him since that day in his apartment, and my emotions were out of control. I took a deep breath and said hi. He wanted to know what was wrong. I explained about Timmy finding his birth certificate and what had happened since then. He was silent then said, "I need to let this sink in. It's caught me off guard."

I became very angry. "Tug, you and I both knew about this. This child is only 11 and it's a complete shock to him. He wants to see his father. I don't want anything from you. You made your choice back in 1966. I've never bothered you, but this is for my son." There was a long pause and he said he would call me back. We hung up.

I was so mad I just sat there. When I calmed down, I went out into the restaurant, got a cup of tea and talked with Shirly. I didn't mention the call to Timmy. I thought it was better for Timmy to think that Tug didn't respond because he didn't get the message than to have him feel even more rejected. Two days later Tug called again. He said he had talked it over with his wife, Phyllis. He told me that she had known about the child before they were married. They both decided to do it for Timmy.

"Not for you or me, Betty. I'll do it for the kid," he said. "Refer to me as Tug to Timmy, and not his father from now on. Now, where's the closest place that we play ball to where you live?"

"I guess Houston," I answered.

He put me on hold. "We'll be in Houston in two weeks, Monday through Thursday. Can you and Timmy come?"

"Yes, I think so."

"I'll send you plane tickets and make hotel reservations."

"No, that won't be necessary. I'll take care of all that myself," I said firmly. We said good-bye and hung up.

After I hung up the phone I started crying. My friend Shirly came in. I told her what Tug had said. I said, "I'll have to take a few days off." I'd never been to Houston. She called our boss, and he and his wife came to the restaurant. I told them the whole story, and they were very supportive. My boss told me to talk to Timmy's school and take care of him being away for a few days. The principal was very nice and said there would be no problem with Timmy being off, just to make sure we brought him back an autographed baseball (which we did).

Those next two weeks were awful, I couldn't eat or sleep. I'd been the only parent to my son for all those years and now his famous, rich father was about to make an appearance. It scared me to death. How was he going to react to Timmy? How was Timmy going to react to Tug? How was I going to react?

My boss Hank and his wife, Tickle, came to the office. Hank gave me directions, and then handed me $200 and hugged me and told me to be careful and call if I needed anything. Tickle hugged me and off we went. It was a six-hour drive. Timmy and I drove our old 1970 Buick, because we couldn't afford to fly.

Timmy was beside himself with excitement. He had brought along his ball and glove and a Phillies jersey we had bought him before we left. He couldn't believe he was

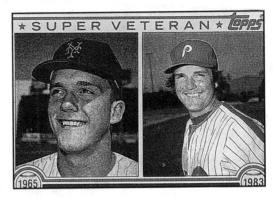

★ SUPER VETERAN ★ Topps

1965 · 1983

CERTIFICATE OF LIVE BIRTH

BIRTH No. 117 67018623

McAthaw

1a. Child's Last Name	1b. First Name	1c. Second Name
~~Smith~~ McGraw	Samuel	Timothy
2. Sex—Girl or Boy?	3. This Birth	4. If Twin or Triplet, Was Child Born	5. Date Of Birth
Boy	Single ☒ Twin ☐ Triplet ☐	1st ☐ 2d ☐ 3d ☐	Month Day Year May 1,1967
6. Place of Birth (City, Town, or Location)	ALTERED JAN 14 1988	CO# 8792 HP; D.C. (2-6-84) OUACHITA, LA.	6b. Parish
Delhi			Richland
6c. Name of Hospital or Institution—(If not in Hospital or Institution give street address or location)			6d. Is Place of Birth Inside City Limits? Yes ☒ No ☐
Delhi Clinic & Sanitarium			
7a. Usual Residence of Mother (City, Town or Location)	7b. Parish	7c. State
Winnsboro	Franklin	La.
7d. Street Address—(If rural indicate location)	7e. Is Residence Inside City Limits? Yes ☐ No ☒	7f. Is Residence on a Farm? Yes ☒ No ☐
Route 4 Box 79		
8. Full Name of Father		9. Color or Race of Father white
Samuel Timothy McGraw (Tug)		
10a. Usual Occupation of Father	10b. Kind of Industry or Business	11. Birthplace, City and State or Foreign Country	12. Age of Father (At time of this birth)
Pro Baseball Player	Sports	New York, New York	22
13. Maiden Name of Mother		14. Color or Race of Mother white
Elizabeth Ann Dagastino		
15. Birthplace of Mother, City and State or Foreign Country	Count Order 13,466 ALTERED APR 29 '74 LL	16. Age of Mother (At time of this birth) 19
Washington D.C.		
17. Previous Deliveries to Mother (Do NOT include this birth)		0		
a. How many OTHER Children are now living? 0	b. How many OTHER Children were born alive But are now Dead? 0	c. How many fetal deaths (fetuses born dead) at ANY time after conception? 0
I certify that the above stated information is true and correct to the best of my knowledge.	18. Signature of Parent or Other Informant Mrs. S.T. McGraw	Parent ☒ Other ☐	19. Date of Signature 5-6-67
Mother's Mailing Address			
Route 4 Box 79 Winnsboro, La.	71295		
I certify that I attended this birth and that the child was born alive on the date stated above.	21. Signature of Attendant Samuel P. Sumem m.	M.D. ☒ Midwife ☐ Other ☐	22. Date of Signature 5/6/67
Date accepted by Local Registrar May 9, 1967	24. Signature of Local Registrar A. Cacicia per D. L. Guin	23. Date filed by State Registrar MAY 15 1967

FOR MEDICAL AND HEALTH USE ONLY

JAN 19 1988

I CERTIFY THAT THIS IS A TRUE AND CORRECT COPY OF A CERTIFICATE
OR DOCUMENT REGISTERED WITH THE VITAL RECORDS REGISTRY OF
THE STATE OF LOUISIANA, PURSUANT TO LSA - R.S. 40:32, ET SEQ.

STATE HEALTH OFFICER   STATE REGISTRAR

Cards of Tug from Tim's
bedroom wall

Betty and Shirly

going to meet Tug McGraw and that he was his father!
When we got to Houston, I called Tug's room. He said he
would meet us in the lobby in one hour. I took a bath while
Timmy went for a swim in the pool. We got dressed and
headed to the lobby. I knew I would recognize Tug, because
of all the press he got and commercials he was in, but I
wondered if he would recognize me. Timmy stayed outside
so I could see Tug first, in case he wanted to talk before he
met Timmy. He walked right up to me. (I remember thinking what an ugly sports coat he had on.) He shook my hand
and said, "Okay, so where's the kid?"

I opened the door and called for Timmy. When Timmy
walked through the door, I couldn't say anything. I had tears
in my eyes. Tug stuck out his hand Timmy shook his hand
and said, "Hi, I'm Timmy." It was all I could do to contain
the tears.

Tug said, "I made arrangements for us to sit in the next
room and talk." Tug and Timmy sat down across from each
other. I just kept looking back and forth at the two of them.
I hadn't realized how much they looked alike. Timmy had
his dad's nose and mouth. They even had the same way of
standing.

I thought Tug handled the conversation very well. They
talked about baseball first. Timmy told Tug that Greg
Luzinski was his favorite Philly. Then Tug said, "Your
mom says you're having problems in school." Timmy shook
his head. "You know, Timmy, sometimes life doesn't give
us all a fair shake, but we live with what we've got. I can't
be a father to you, but I can be a friend. It looks like your
mom has done a terrific job, and you've got a terrific mom,
who I know loves you very much. So look this thing
straight in the eye and go on. From now on, just say we're

friends." He then asked Timmy if he wanted to see a ball
game. Timmy said, "Yeah!"

Before we left, Tug got me aside and said, "If anyone
should ask, you are an old friend and I'm showing your son
a good time."

"Of course," I answered.

That afternoon we went to the park for batting practice.
Timmy went down to the dugout, and Tug gave him a cap
and ball signed by the whole team. He took Timmy on the
field while I sat up in the stands and watched. Timmy
played catch with his hero, Greg Luzinski. He'd turn and
wave to me. (I was wishing I had borrowed a camera to
take pictures of him.) My heart was pounding and I was
very nervous—very emotional. How can Timmy be happy?
I thought. I have nothing. His father has an entirely different
way of life . . . a dream life. It scared me. I couldn't give
him as much, but I surely loved him more than anyone possibly could. I hoped Timmy knew that. I always tried to
show and tell all my children how much I loved them all the
time.

While Timmy was in the dugout one of the players came
over to the fence and motioned for me. I walked over and
he asked, "You and Tug old friends?"

"Yes we are."

"How long?"

"About twelve years."

"And, how old is your son?" he questioned.

"Eleven."

"I thought so." With that he just walked off. He could
see the outstanding resemblance.

After the game we went back to the hotel. Tug called
about an hour later to see how it went. I told him Timmy

had had a great time. He really enjoyed all the excitement.
"Good," Tug said. "Now, Betty, you need to stop referring
to me as Timmy's father and just let this all pass. If you
stop saying I'm his father, he'll be able to deal with it better." I couldn't believe what he had just said. I hung up on
him. I couldn't say anything to him. He was only thinking
of himself, not our son. The next day, we were supposed to
meet Tug for lunch and then drive home. We met him in the
hotel restaurant. Tug ordered a burger and chocolate shake.
So did Timmy. I looked at Timmy and sort of laughed because he usually drank vanilla shakes, and he was not too
crazy about chocolate. I guess he wanted to be like his "father."

The talk of the day was baseball and Little League, small
talk between an adult and a child. After an hour, we said
our good-byes and left. I had nothing more to say to Tug.
He had said it all the night before. Of course I didn't say
anything to Timmy about the previous night's conversation.
Timmy was on cloud nine and couldn't wait to get home
and tell his best friend, Lance, about everything. He had
gotten Lance and the principal a ball with Tug's autograph,
and for himself, he had one with the whole team's auto-
graphs, plus the Phillies hat that Tug had given him.

Things seemed to go better for Timmy after that and he
started adjusting better to the situation. He did ask, however,
if he could use the name McGraw. I said, "Sure. It is your
name." At that point, Timmy Smith became Tim McGraw.
He also said he thought he was now too old to be called
Timmy. He liked Tim better. Maybe he wanted a new first
name to go with his new last name. (It's funny that although
Tug was not around in Tim's childhood days when we
called him Timmy, and met him the year he decided he was

too old to be called that. To this day, he still calls Tim Tim-my.)

Tim wrote letters to Tug in care of the Phillies' office all the time. That's the only address we had. When I got my phone bill the next month, there were two calls to the Phi-llies. I asked Tim about them, and he said he had tried to call Tug. But just as the letters received no response, the phone calls were also ignored. The next year when school started, Tim decided to use Smith as his last name. He wasn't comfortable using McGraw since he never heard from his dad despite all his attempts to establish a relation-ship. It broke my heart seeing Tim watch every televised Phillies' game just hoping to catch a glimpse of his dad. He always read the sports pages, as well, to try to keep tabs on Tug's career.

Chapter 14

Our life went on with little change. Tim finally quit trying to communicate with Tug and continued on with his life. He really got into basketball. It became the sport of choice for him. Oh, he still loved baseball but was focusing more on basketball and was a good player. Whether it was a shield or not, I don't really know. He went to basketball camp in the summer, and he and the girls went to 4H camp. Living in a rural area, they all belonged to 4H.

I worked so much that there was little time for socializing. So when I did, it was a big deal; everyone acted as if it were a major event. I went out with friends. I really didn't date; I didn't have time with work and the kids. Cathy and I would go to the movies or she would come over to my house and we'd cook and watch movies. Cathy, Bubba and Shirly, my friends from work, were the ones I spent the most time with. I had never done a lot of dating in high school. Jimmy was my steady date, and then after Tim was born, I didn't have the time and was just too tired. I dated a little before I married Horace but only a few times.

Then I met Gregg. He was the first guy I really dated. Gregg was a cowboy . . . *a real cowboy*. He was in college and participated in all the rodeos. I met him one afternoon in the lounge at work. I was helping the bartender because the hostess was running late. Gregg walked into the lounge that afternoon. He was tall and slim and wore a cowboy hat and Wranglers. He was a real nice looking cowboy. I was 29 and he was 25. He knew the bartender, so he asked him to introduce us. The three of us had been talking a few minutes when the hostess arrived. I excused myself so I could go home to my kids.

A few days later as I was sitting in my office, one of the waitresses came to the door and said "There's a guy in the dining room wanting to see you, and he said to tell you he's buying you lunch." Since this wasn't a regular occurrence, my curiosity got the best of me and I walked into the restaurant. Imagine my surprise at seeing the "cowboy" sitting there motioning for me to join him. I sat down and we began talking. Shirly, the restaurant manager, came over, obviously wanting to be introduced to Gregg. She invited herself to join us, and we had a very pleasant lunch. The conversation just flowed.

Gregg asked me to dinner that night, but I declined. He was persistent. Finally I said, "Why would you want to take an old lady with three kids to dinner?"

"Well, old ladies get hungry too. You do eat, don't you?" he replied. We laughed and I thanked him but still declined. After lunch, he left.

Shirly said, "Girl, you're crazy. He's adorable."

"Yeah, and young," I answered.

"Not much younger then you," Shirly said.

I replied as I walked away, "Only in years, honey. I have miles over that boy."

About a week later, my friend Betty Jo wanted to go the Rusty Nail Lounge and asked me if I would go with her. My babysitter was able to keep the kids, so we went to hear the great house band the lounge had. The band, James Pastel and Company, was very popular, and the Rusty Nail was the hottest club in town then. I was really surprised to see

Gregg there. He saw me come in and came over and sat with us for a little while. When Gregg went to the bar, Betty Jo commented on how cute he was. He tried all night to get me to dance, but I wouldn't. He even tried to get Betty Jo to make me dance. I just felt so uncomfortable around him; I felt "old."

About two weeks later, as I sat at home watching television with the kids, someone knocked at the door. I answered and to my shock, it was none other than Gregg. "How did you know where I lived?" I asked. (We lived 20 miles in the country.)

"Bubba told me," Gregg said.

I invited him in, thinking I would deal with Bubba soon, and introduced him to my kids. He talked about rodeos with the kids. Tim went to get his cowboy hat to show him. Within 30 minutes, Gregg had invited the kids to a rodeo. I gave him the "look"—you know the one! Of course, the kids started screaming and jumping up and down. He said, "Well, I've got tickets, but you're going to have to talk your mom into it. It's this Saturday night." The kids begged and begged until I finally gave in. Then I told them to go to bed.

Then I said, "Okay, Gregg, it's time for you to go home, too." I walked him to the door and told him I'd get even.

He gave me a peck on the cheek and said, "Maybe, but I won this time. Now, you're going on a date with me."

I looked at him and said, "Don't think you've won. This isn't a date." He turned and laughed and got into his truck waving good-bye. I couldn't help thinking about him and how I was going to kill Bubba!

The next day when Bubba came in to open the lounge, I was waiting for him. I said, "Bubba, come here. What do you mean giving my address to someone?"

He laughed and said, "Hey, you only told me never to

give your phone number out. Come on, Betty, he's a nice guy and you'll have a good time. You need some fun and romance in your life." (You know, Bubba was right.)

I was surprised to find myself looking forward to Saturday night. Friday, I got off work at 3 p.m. so I could get home early. The kids wanted to go skating. I hadn't been home long when Gregg drove up.

"Hey, Bubba said you left early today," he said. "Is something wrong? I went by the restaurant because I wanted to take you to get the kids cowboy shirts and hats for the rodeo."

"Nothing's wrong. I have plans with the kids. Besides, I can't let you do that." By this time the kids had seen Gregg and had come outside.

"But I really want to buy your kids some shirts and hats," he said. Once again, he made the statement in front of the kids, and they pestered me until I finally gave in. I warned the kids they would be late for skating, but skating no longer mattered. It was obvious to me that they missed having a man around wanting to do things with them, so we all went shopping. I don't know who had a better time, Gregg or the kids. When he dropped us off that evening, he said he would pick us up at seven the following night.

All day Saturday, the kids were excited about going to the rodeo. Horace always went to the rodeos, but the kids had only been once. (They hadn't seen much of Horace lately.) Gregg was very prompt (or anxious) and picked us up right at 7 p.m. I felt so old around him, even though there was only a four year difference in our ages. When we got to our seats, every college kid Gregg knew must have been sitting beside us. I was so embarrassed.

The kids loved the rodeo. They had a ball. Afterward, Gregg suggested we all go eat. I agreed, thinking we would be going to Burger King. Instead, he took us to the restaurant where I worked. All the college kids that were sitting around us at the rodeo were there sitting at a long table and insisted on us joining them. I felt like a mother hen with all her chicks. I don't know how I got through that night.

Gregg started showing up every weekend to fix things around the house and play football with Tim. He really got very involved with my kids; they really liked each other. It got to be close to Christmas, and Gregg and I were still seeing each other. I always took Christmas week off for my vacation to get ready—I liked to bake and make personal gifts. Christmas was always my favorite time of the year and still is; the kids and I always had a big time. They loved buying gifts for friends and making decorations and cookies. We always decorated the whole house, and Tim would hang lights outside and wrap the plants out front in lights. We would go caroling, and always they'd have friends over. Christmas was great! This year, instead of buying a tree, Gregg decided he and the kids would go in the woods and cut one. They went all over until dark looking and ended up buying one that night on the way home since they couldn't find that perfect tree. We were up till midnight trimming it.

Most of the nights during that week we played games like Monopoly. One night I was making cocoa and fixing a plate of cookies when I heard Gregg ask the kids what they were getting for Christmas. Tim said, "I asked Santa for a guitar and BB gun."

Tracey said, "I want skates and a new basketball."

Sandy said, "I just want baby dolls."

Lance, Tim's best friend, laughed and said, "They still believe in Santa" to Gregg.

Tim said in a quiet voice, "Lance stop. You know Mom. We have to pretend."

Tracey said, "Hush! Mom's in the kitchen. She won't let anyone say there's no Santa. So you pretend and talk about him like he's real. Mom said when you don't believe, Santa does not come and see you! So, we play along . . . it's her game."

Tim said, "I think she really believes in Santa." They all laughed. "She loves Christmas, the real old fashioned Christmas," Tim explained. "She even makes us go caroling. We always have fun, and we leave cookies and milk for Santa!" (I still love the real meaning of Christmas and still make the kids talk about Santa).

For Christmas that year, Gregg bought me a beautiful sweater and watch. He was just such a nice guy. He got Tim his BB gun, Tracey her skates and Sandy a doll. I got Tim his first guitar, Tracey a basketball and Sandy another doll. Sandy had started collecting dolls at an early age and she still does. Christmas came and went. During the holidays, I had watched Gregg with my kids. They really enjoyed him. I knew I was getting more interested, so I needed to step back and look at this situation. Was this the best thing for everybody?

I always tried to have things for the kids to do. I'd let them invite their friends for cookouts and have parties from time to time. I liked for them to stay home as much as possible, but I wanted them to have fun. We always had a gang at our house, and I still do. My kids adopt everybody. When you're their friend, you're part of our family. I guess that's why I've always got a full house all the time. We are just a loving family. We do a lot of hugging. (I have a habit of hugging people; that's just me.)

It was getting to be spring, close to my birthday. Shirly, Cathy and Bubba planned a birthday party for me. My boss and his wife, some of my friends and even my sister from

Texas came. Gregg gave me a pretty pair of diamond earrings. They were beautiful, but this relationship was bothering me. I enjoyed him being around, and the kids sure did too, but it worried me. It wasn't fair to him. He needed someone younger, someone his age, not a ready-made family. He needed his own children. (Remember, I had cancer surgery and could not have any more children. I knew if I was his mother that would bother me.) So I told Gregg we needed to stop seeing each other and to just be friends. He didn't agree, so I told him my reasons. He said, "Shouldn't I make that decision?"

"No, you won't listen to me," I said. We stopped dating for a while. He'd come around and call and we'd talk. He finally stopped calling. He did call however, when he found a girlfriend and told me all about her. I was glad and sad. I have to admit, I really liked him. But this was for the best. I hope he found that special girl.

Tracey, Tim and Sandy

Chapter 15

Tim didn't mentioned Tug for a while. He stayed busy with school, sports, and his friends. He got his driver's license and I let him drive the car. Now he could take the girls places; that was a big help to me.

When Tim was 15, he started riding in rodeos. He had become an accomplished rider. (In fact all my kids are very good riders.) He did heading and heeling with his friend, Tim Watson. (For those of you not in the know, heading and heeling is when two riders rope one cow, one rider at the head and one at the feet.) He always came home after rodeos and said, "Mom, I sure want to ride the bulls or those broncos."

I'd say, "No, indeed, boy! I don't want you to be mangled for life."

"Oh Mom, it's cool and the girls really dig those bull riders."

"No sir! No way, Tim. That's the end of that subject."

One late night I was in my room, and it was about time for Tim to come home. He had been to a rodeo in Shreveport, about two hours away, and it had rained all night. Tim was almost 16 then. I heard him come in and go straight to the bathroom and start the shower. I could hear him groaning. When he came out of the bathroom, I met him in the hall and said, "What's wrong, Tim?"

"Mom, don't be mad, but I did something I shouldn't have. I'm sorry."

"What Tim? What did you do?"

"I signed your name so I could ride the bucking horses. Mom, when that horse bucked, he threw me straight up in the air and I thought I'd never see the ground again. I swear, I'll never do that again." I couldn't help but laugh. He wasn't hurt, but he sure was sore. After that, I made sure I went with him to most of his rodeos, but I let him ride what he wanted. He did well and even won a couple of second and third place belt buckles.

One day while I was working in my rose bed, Betty Jo came over and we talked outside for a while. I told her about Tim and the rodeo incident. We laughed and then went inside to make coffee. We were talking, as all mothers do, about our kids. I told her how Tim had helped me with my rose garden. He was a business man by age 11. The kids got $5 a week allowance; for his, Timmy had to clean his room and take out the garbage. (He was paid extra for other odd jobs.) One time I told him I needed seven holes dug in my rose bed and I'd give him a dollar a hole. When I got home from work they were dug. So I changed clothes and went out to plant my roses. A neighbor boy, a year younger than Tim, came over looking for him. I said he was playing ball. He said, "Well, Tim owes me $3.50, and I wanted to collect my money." I asked why Tim owed him money. He informed me that he had dug the holes for fifty cents a hole and had come by to collect. My little entrepreneur—always thinking. He always told me he wasn't going to be a blue-collar worker. He was going to work in an office and be a millionaire before he was thirty.

We laughed and the girls came in. They wanted to know what was so funny. I told Tracey the story I had just told Betty Jo. She said, "Tim's always done that. He'll give me and Sandy some of his allowance to clean his room for him.

He says, 'Why work hard if you don't have to?' He wants to be a lawyer or an actor. He says you have to have a little actor in you to be a lawyer."

"Tracey, what do you want to be?" I asked.

"Just out of school."

"How about you, Sandy?"

"I'm going to be a mom. I don't want to do anything else."

"Well, get married and have a husband first," Betty Jo said.

Sandy laughed and went outside. I told Betty Jo I just wanted my kids to be happy and have things be better for them.

The next day I was in the kitchen ironing. Sandy and Tracey were cleaning their room, and Tim was in his room, supposedly cleaning it, but I knew better than that. He always bribed his sisters to do it by the end of the day, so I'd let him go to town. He came out of his room with the newspaper. "Look Mom," he said. It was an article on Tug. I said I would read it when I was through. Tim started talking about college. "Mom, I know you can't afford college for me," he began.

Before he could finish his sentence, I said, "Honey, don't worry, there are all kinds of scholarships and student loans. We can get you one, and you can go to college if you want to."

"Listen, Mom, Tug makes a lot of money. I know you said you never wanted to bother him or ask him for anything because you didn't want to interfere and maybe hurt his career, but he's retiring now. Why can't you ask him to just send me to college? That's fair, isn't it? After all, he never paid any child support or did anything for you or me." Then he handed me the paper. The article announced Tug's retire-

Tim, Junior Choir

Tracey at prom time at their
home in Start

ment. "See, he's retiring. He's leaving his career, so now it couldn't hurt him!"

What could I say? "Well, Tim, I don't know. I guess we could ask him," I answered.

Tim and I sat down and wrote a long letter to Tug. We sent it to the Phillies' office. In the letter, I told Tug that Tim had approached me with this question and asked if he could possibly pay for his son's college education. He had not paid child support of any kind, or even sent a birthday or Christmas card. Could he please think about this? We mailed the letter and waited, but we didn't get a response.

We all went on with our lives. We kind of put Tug on the back burner. I figured we probably wouldn't hear from him. Even though Tug was retiring, I'd still catch Tim checking the sports section for information about him. But I never said anything. We just went about our everyday lives with work, school, church and the kids' extra activities like basketball, baseball, football and of course skating on Friday nights.

Then one day Tim mentioned something about Tug. "Mom, did you ever hear anything from Tug," he asked. I said no, not yet. He looked disappointed but didn't say anything. Months went by with no answer. I wrote a second time. It was now the summer before Tim's senior year, and we still hadn't heard anything. Tim was hurt about not hearing from Tug. He didn't say much to me, but he did to his friend Lance and his sisters. I have a slow-burning temper, but this treatment of my son made me angry. Then I did something I never thought I would do.

My friend Cathy was over at our house one Sunday, and I was telling her about the letter to Tug. She got angry at me. "Betty, listen, this isn't fair to Tim," she said. "That man is his father. Timmy should not be worrying about you

working so hard to send him to college. His father owes it
to him. You've supported him for almost 18 years. Now it's
his father's turn."

"You can go to the HRS office," she continued. "They
will figure what Tug owes you in back child support.
They'll collect it for you and then you can send Tim to college yourself, with your money. There will probably be
enough to make life a little easier for you."

We talked for a long, long time. It took a lot of talking,
but she convinced me. So that Monday, Cathy and I went
downtown to the HRS office and told the caseworker the
story. He said first we needed an address. I gave him the
Philadelphia Phillies' address. The he said we needed some
information: a Social Security number or something to
check income. I told him all I had was a newspaper article.
The clipping said Tug had signed a contract for $1.5 million
a year. The caseworker said he would take care of it and
that it would take a few weeks for things to get started.

Cathy and I went back to the office. We went in the restaurant; she got a cup of coffee and I got a cup of tea. We
just sat there. I didn't say anything for a while.

She asked, "Betty, are you okay?"

I had tears in my eyes. I said, "Cathy, I just hope this
doesn't make Tug mad. I always stayed away and let him
be. I never wanted to do anything that would make him hate
Tim. I realized a long time ago that he didn't care about me
and I can handle that, but I couldn't take him turning on
Tim."

She said, "Don't worry. He doesn't have contact with
Tim now, so what can it hurt? You're doing the right thing.
Remember that you're not the bad guy here!"

About two weeks passed and then I got a phone call. It
was an attorney in Boston. He said he worked for Tug. He

wanted to know why I was filing a suit with the state for nonsupport. Tim was 17. Why now? I explained about the letters and Tim wanting to go to college and our income and lifestyle. We talked for a while and he said, "So, I'm getting the feeling we could probably settle this without going to court?"

I said, "I never wanted to go to court. I don't need Tug McGraw, but my son does need to go to college. He's smart; he makes straight A's and he wants to go on to college."

The lawyer wanted to know if I would drop the papers with the state. I said I would as soon as I knew Tug would pay for college. He said he'd call me back in a few days. I hung up the phone feeling scared. It was basically me against a Boston law firm, and I felt whipped already.

A few days later Tug's lawyer called back, told me to go ahead and get figures together and then we would go from there. I called Cathy. She and I went to the college and got figures. We did a lot of hemming and hawing back and forth, and then they gave us their final offer. Tim wanted to go to law school, so that meant seven years of school. I wanted to get enough for school and for him to have some extra money for himself. They came up with a payment plan for seven years. I asked for a car for Tim, but they decided against that. I sat down and went over the offer with Tim. It had a clause preventing Tim from ever contacting Tug or any member of his family.

"Do you understand what that means?" I asked. "You have a half-brother and sister you cannot contact, and you'll never see Tug again."

Tim didn't see that he was giving up much. He'd only seen Tug once, at his own urging. "So what am I losing, Mom? As for my brother and sister, when they turn 21, they can decide if they want to know me. I can contact them, and they can decide.'' The only other thing he wanted was to see Tug one more time. I asked him why. He said he didn't know. Maybe he just wanted to punch Tug in the nose. Finally, we all agreed on the terms and signed the papers.

Tug agreed to the meeting. He offered to pay for us to come out to Houston, and this time I agreed. (I guess Houston was a neutral territory.) Tim and I walked into a very elegant hotel. Tim was 17 years old and six feet tall—a nice-looking boy, very well mannered. (All my kids are well mannered.)

I saw Tug standing at the desk and said, "Tim, there is your father." We walked up to Tug and Tim tapped him on the shoulder. He turned and said, "Hey, where is the . . . boy?" His eyes were looking down at about the height of an 11-year-old. He had to look up to find Tim. Tim was now taller than Tug. This was the second time I'd seen him since the night I got pregnant. He still looked good. There's something youthful about him, even now. Tug doesn't look his age, and he sure doesn't act it. Tim's more mature than he is.

Tim and I had adjoining suites. He couldn't get over the hotel. There was a phone in the bathroom and a mall right inside the hotel! Quite a difference from Start, Louisiana. Tim was in awe. He said, "I wonder what this costs." I said I surely didn't know. Tim was curious. He called down to the desk and found out the suite cost $185 a night—almost as much as I took home in a week—and he was just fascinated. He couldn't believe it.

Tug was just as incredulous later when we met for lunch and he found out that Tim had been offered several scholarships and had chosen the one for music. He had no idea they gave out scholarships for singing. It was completely beyond his ken. He said, "Betty, I guess that's your side of him coming out." I told Tim and Tug that they would be going out to dinner by themselves that night. They needed to get to know each other and I needed to buy souvenirs for my girls.

About 10:30 that night, I was back in my room looking over my purchases when I heard a loud banging on my door. There they were, Tug and Tim, arms around each other's shoulders, giggling like a couple of kids. "Hey, Betty," Tug said. "Tim and I have come to an understanding."

"Okay, I said. "And what may I ask is that?"

"I'm Tim's dad and he's my son."

"No kidding, Sherlock. Aren't you the smart one?"

"Really, he's just like me. He loves sports. He looks like me. He's great. I don't know where the singing thing comes from."

I said, "Excuse me. He is my son also, and I can sing, you know!" They laughed.

Tug said, "I don't know how to do it yet, and Phyllis won't like it, but I want to get to know Tim and I want him to meet Mark and Carrie. They don't even know they have a brother. But we'll work it out. Forget those papers—that's just lawyers. I'll still send the money for college." We all hugged and that was that.

Tug left and Tim and I talked a long time. He was excited. I was glad, nervous and oh so scared. I knew he was almost grown, but I couldn't face losing my son. He'd been all mine for 17 years. I was scared to death. But I really was glad they had hit it off and seemed to like each other. We flew home the next morning. Tim, again, didn't hear from Tug. Of course I kept those papers. I was going to make sure I had money for college.

Tim didn't hear anything at all from Tug after we got

home. I saw on my phone bills that he called Tug a couple
of times at his lawyer's office. In April I sent Tug an invita-
tion to Tim's graduation at his lawyer's address. (That's all
I had.)

We didn't hear anything, so I called Tug's attorney to see
if he might come for graduation. He said no because someone might recognize him. So he really hadn't meant what he
said, if he was afraid of being recognized. I didn't tell Tim.
(Again, no word from him was better than hearing this.)

Tim 11th grade

Tim's senior
picture

Tim in his high school
football uniform

Betty at Tim's high
school graduation

Tracey, Tim and Sandy at
Tim's graduation

Chapter 16

Graduation day came, and Tim was salutatorian, with the second highest grade point average of his high school class. He was supposed to give a speech. I stayed after him all day and finally about 30 minutes before the ceremony, he sat down and wrote it. Tracey rewrote it while he was taking a shower so he would be able to read it. It was a wonderful day—my first child's graduation. I was so proud, as were his sisters and grandparents.

Tim enrolled in college. Sandy was in the ninth grade, and Tracey was getting ready for her senior year. Tim was still living at home, but as usual he had some guys from school at the house all the time. He was singing with a group called the Electones. They did concerts at school and sang at the fair. We all went to the fair and invited the choir director from church. Tim sang "I.O.U.," a Lee Greenwood hit. He had all the girls screaming (even then). Patsy, our choir director, started laughing and said, "Just think, he grew up singing in church, and now girls are screaming."

Sandy wasn't doing well in school. I'd tried to help her more with her homework. She was passing, but barely. Tracey was homecoming queen that year. She sure was pretty. I don't think she expected to win, because she sure looked surprised.

One day I was cleaning house when the phone rang. It was two weeks before Easter. I answered the phone, and it was Tug. "Hey Betty, it's me, Tug."

"Hello Tug," I said hesitating.

"So how are you?" he said.

"I'm fine, thank you, and how are you," I replied.

He said, "I'm great . . . listen, I think it's time Tim met his stepmom and brother and sister. What do you think?"

I didn't say anything for a minute. Then I answered, "Well, I guess it is about time!"

He then said "Can I talk to Tim?" I said, "He's not here right now. He's coaching his little RA basketball team in a game at church. Can I have him call you?"

"Sure," Tug said. He then said he wanted to fly Tim and one of his friends to the Phillies' training camp in Florida and meet him, his wife and kids for the Easter weekend. "So what do you think? Will he want to go?" he asked.

Tug really sounded excited. I got that nervous feeling again. It's hard to explain, that glad but sad kind of sickening in my stomach. I guess I knew things were going to change, and that scared me. "I think he will," I answered. "He'll probably want to bring Lance. I'll ask Lance's parents and tell Tim. Lance is with him now. Give me your number." He gave me the number. Then we said good-bye and hung up.

Tracey, Sandy and I left to go tell Tim. We walked into the gym, and I told Tim that Tug had called and what he had said. He was in a state of disbelief and shock. His best friend, Lance, was with him. Both boys looked at each other and started giving each other "high fives" and grinning from ear to ear. I went by to see Lance's mom on the way home to ask if Lance could go. They were excited and agreed.

Neither boy had ever been away from home except for camp. Tim had only flown that one time to see Tug, and Lance had never been in a plane. The boys were beside themselves with excitement. So two weeks later, Tim and Lance left for Florida. Lance's mom and I took the boys to the airport. Lance was nervous about flying, but Tim was acting like an old pro.

Tim called me from Florida, saying how much he liked his brother and sister and that Tug's wife was very nice. "Mom, she reminds me of you." He said. "She talks a lot."

"Very funny, Mr. Tim!" I said. He also said that Carrie looked a lot like him and that Mark was great. (We've all gotten to know Mark well since then. He's a sweet person. He visits us now and then and has even spent a few Thanksgivings with us. We haven't gotten to know Carrie very well. She's only been around a few times.)

The boys were gone two days. When they got home they told us about the Phillies' camp and all about the trip. Tim said Tug's wife, Phyllis, invited him to come visit.

The day after Tim got home, I got a call from Phyllis. She thanked me for letting Tim come and meet them. She said, "He is a wonderful boy, Betty. You've done a great job raising him." I thanked her. She said they would like Tim to come visit when school was out. I told her if he wanted to we would work it out. Then we just chatted about all the kids. I think we talked for two hours.

After a while, Tim finally got back down to earth. Tim called Tug and his family from time to time but he didn't visit again until the next year. Mark, Tim's half-brother, stayed in touch with Tim occasionally. Tim called his dad a few times and visited on a weekend every now and then, but they didn't really establish a relationship for several more years.

Tim and Tug's daughter Carrie

Tug's son Mark, Tim and Tug

Chapter 17

This brings me to a very unhappy part of my life. I probably should title this chapter "stupid," because I was! This is one part of my life I have tried to forget completely, but I can't. My children have tried to forget as well. It took a long time for me to decide whether or not to write about this. This chapter is out of sequence. This man was in my life before, but I decided to tell this story all at one time and get it over with. I'm only going to refer to him as "he" or "him."

The reason I choose not to use his name in my book is out of respect for his children. Anyone from the very small town where we lived who reads this will know who it is, and his name is not important. It took a long time for me to write this part. This is ugly. He hurt one of my daughters, and as you read this you will see how easily a person can be blinded. The old clichés "a wolf in sheep's clothing" and "you can't judge a book by its cover" fit. He completely fooled me. I felt responsible. After all, I took this man into my home; I married him.

He was one of the two cops who would answer the domestic calls when Horace had his blow-ups. He was tall, dark and very handsome. He was of Hispanic descent with an olive complexion and piercing brown eyes. The other cop was black and a great guy. Horace accused me of having an affair with them, especially him. (But, then again, Horace always accused me of having affairs with everyone who even spoke to me.) I never did. Not while Horace and I were married. I was divorced several months before he started showing up in my life. I would run into him at the Little League Ball Park, where he was one of the coaches. He had a son younger than Tim who played ball. I'd also see him having coffee at the restaurant where I worked. He would always talk to me and flirt with me, and I was flattered by his attention; after all, here was this very nice-looking man paying attention to me. I guess I couldn't believe someone that good-looking would be interested in me. When Little League was over, I missed the attention that he gave me. It really did wonders for my self-esteem. I only wish now that I had never met him.

He would pop up from time to time even when I was dating Gregg. Eventually we did get involved after his continuous pursuit over a number of years. When this man began trying to court me, I was very flattered. I just fell, and fell hard! I loved this man. I didn't think I would ever trust a man again. I had heard rumors, but I didn't listen. I chose to believe those rumors were just small-town gossip. There was something about him that wouldn't let me let go of him. Even my mother didn't like him. She thought he was a womanizer, but I wouldn't believe it. You never do when you're in love. We dated off and on in the beginning. More off than on. He was in a bad marriage when I met him, and he and his wife separated frequently. He finally left his wife, moved in with his parents and got a divorce.

We then became an item. He had children around the same age as mine, and he was great with my kids at first. We were like the Brady Bunch. He had three and I had three, and we did things together as a family. That he seemed to like my kids is what did it for me. I'd look at him and smile, thinking this is it. I was hooked. He had cast his spell on me. After several years of dating, we decided to get married. I sat the kids down one evening and told them that we wanted to get married and asked their feelings. They thought it was great and said they just wanted me to be happy. The next day I went to my mom's to tell her. Naturally, she wasn't enthusiastic but she said if I was going to do it, then we would be married in her home. We planned a small wedding with just a few family members and friends. Shirly was my matron of honor. Cathy, Regina and my kids were there. His ex-wife would not let their kids come, but his mom and dad were there. We went on a short honeymoon with Shirly and her husband. We went deep-sea fishing. I have motion sickness and wasn't very comfortable, but we did have a good time. I had never had a vacation before, so it was great.

When we got back from the honeymoon, I went back to work and we all began adjusting to our new life. Soon after we married, he began changing. He wasn't as attentive. He was mean to Tim, never wanting to do anything with him. He was not like he had been during the Little League days. Tim ignored him and tried to stay out of his way. We weren't getting along, so I stayed busy with my job. It was Tim's junior year and something was always going on, so I didn't think much about it. My husband spent a lot of time with the girls and their friends playing Monopoly and football, and he spent a lot of time teaching Sandy and his daughter to drive. Things were just different.

He and I were having problems. He was very critical and acted like he had a chip on his shoulder. He was indifferent with the kids. He criticized the way I handled things with Tug. He thought I should have gotten all my back child support and not settled, but it was my decision. Then he began going over to his ex-wife's to see his kids more and more often, sometimes staying until after midnight, when his kids were normally in bed by nine. There was more and more distance between us, and he was just plain mean to my kids. He never wanted them around. He stopped being the affectionate, loving person to me that he had been. I think I realized within a year that this wasn't it either, but I stayed in the marriage, not wanting to put my kids through another divorce. I just began working more and got more involved in my kids' lives and church.

One day I came home to find him very angry. I asked him what was wrong. He told me that he was tired of my damn kids. They wouldn't listen to him. He said he had told Sandy to stay home and clean her room. She wouldn't listen. She left and went to one of her girlfriend's. I had had a hard day and was tired, so I threw my stuff down. Sandy was in Tim's room by that time; I went in there and began getting on to her about not doing what he had told her to do. That's when she said, "I'm not staying in this house when he's here. He won't keep his hands off me!" *Sandy was almost fourteen and fully developed so she looked much older.*

Before I could say anything else, Tim ran and got his shotgun and started running for him. Here I was with a hysterical teenager who was crying and a son with a gun going after my so-called husband. I ran and tackled Tim and took the gun away from him. Tim went in and started swearing at him, calling him all sorts of names. I grabbed Tim and told him to go back and stay with Sandy, that I would be there in a minute. Tracey came out of her room and wanted to know what was going on. I told her to go into Tim's room with Tim and Sandy. They would tell her what was going on. I went in our room, where he was just sitting on the bed. I looked at him and said, "Do you know what Sandy just told me?"

"Yeah, I know," he said. "I'm glad it's all out in the open. I have a problem. I didn't hurt her."

He was so matter-of-fact about it that I just flew into a rage. I don't even remember the names I called him, but I told him that living with Horace Smith was better than this. My being beaten was a lot better than someone hurting my child. That's when he repeated, "I didn't hurt her." I told him he was crazy. He did hurt her, maybe not physically, but certainly on an emotional level. I told him he was a sick human being and to get out of my house. He went to the closet to get his things, but I yelled at him to get out now. I told him I would send him his things, and if he didn't leave now, I would call the police.

He left and I went in to talk to my kids. Tim was so mad he wanted to kill him. I wanted to find out what all he had done to my daughter. I wanted the details. Sandy told me that he had fondled her all over her body several times over the last couple years. I kept asking her if he had done anything else to her. Sandy was my most vulnerable child and might be afraid to tell me everything that he had done to her. She said no. I then asked Tracey if he had ever bothered her. She said absolutely not. She said, "He knows if he ever tried anything with me that I would kick the shit out of him!" (Tracey would. Even though she was built like me, Tracey would not back down from a fight with anyone, regardless of their size.) Sandy, being my baby, was always more vulnerable.

After Sandy and Tracey went to bed, Tim and I talked about what had happened. I told Tim I needed to get out of the house for a few minutes and talk to my friend Shirly. Tim said he would stay with the girls. I went to Shirly's

house and told her what had happened and got my crying
over with. I tried not to cry in front of my kids. Now I felt
totally stupid. How could I have let someone hurt my child
like that? I took Sandy to the doctor the next day, just to be
sure she wasn't holding anything back from me. Things
were becoming more clear to me now. Sandy's behavior had
changed recently. She was getting into trouble at school and
was more headstrong than normal, more defiant. It all made
sense now.

He moved back in with his parents. I sent all his things
over there. His mother called me to see why he was back at
home. I told her what had happened. She didn't believe me.
At that point, I had called one of our best friends from our
church and told her what had happened. She helped me
counsel the kids. It was good to have someone to talk to
other than Shirly.

We asked Sandy if she wanted me to press charges, but
she said no. She didn't want to have to tell anyone about it.
She was also afraid of what her father would do to him if
he found out about it. (She's still scared today of what her
father would do.)

I think that was the last straw when everything came
down on me. I called Mary, and we talked about what had
happened.

"Why don't you come to Florida?" she asked. I told her
I couldn't because Tracey would be graduating soon and she
would want to graduate here. I wasn't going to do anything
except try to help Sandy and make things as normal as possible. Tracey's graduation was right around the corner. I remember losing my senior year, and I would not let that happen to Tracey. I told Mary I would come visit soon.

So our life went on. Sandy didn't handle things very
well. She was different, defiant and stubborn, not a sweet

little girl anymore. We told very few people. I didn't even file for divorce. He could do that. He could pay for it. Naturally the gossip started, which didn't bother me. I heard he was involved with another woman, and that was fine with me. I probably should have listened to the gossip when he quit the police force, but you can't look back. I couldn't believe how this had happened and I hadn't seen it.

His kids had come to our house and his oldest, his wife's by a previous marriage, was a wild child. Thirteen going on 25. You name it, she'd try it. I started having problems with Sandy being unruly about the same time. When she turned 14, she started arguing with me. Her grades were awful. I caught her smoking, and I figured it was his daughter's influence so I said she couldn't come over too often anymore. But that wasn't it. It was him. Why didn't I see it? How could this happen? This hurt my child. I could handle me being hurt. Hell, I've been through all that before. But this was the hardest thing I'd ever had to deal with. I thought I was losing my mind. I hid it as best I could. Sandy did fairly well, but she became so defiant from dealing with what had happened to her.

I tried everything: talking to her, trying to get her to talk to me. I tried my best to let her know it wasn't her fault. She was a child; it's the adult's fault, not the child's. Nothing a child does makes this kind of thing their fault. I was mad at myself. . . . I tried to think about all the signs. How could I have been so stupid to let this man into my home? How could I have loved someone who would hurt a child? I just kept thinking about how stupid I was. There was no other word for it. It's also scary that kind of thing is common all over the world. Life is hard enough. Growing up is painful by itself. A child should not have to go through the pain, embarrassment and shock of this.

He had acted great with my kids; then he stopped. He was good with Tim; then he picked on him a lot and got mad when he wanted to have friends over. In the beginning he was very loving; then he began being distant to me. He didn't work much. While I was working he'd come over to my job and hang around and flirt with the waitresses. Everyone had warned me, even my mother. He was a womanizer, but I didn't believe them; you never do. I guess I was blinded by love. It took me years after that to know what real love is supposed to be, and this wasn't it.

I was never comfortable with him. He always bothered me—I think I knew he'd run around on me just like he did his first wife, but I never dreamed anything like this would happen. When I finally woke up, we were already married, and I wasn't putting my kids through another divorce if I could help it. I made the best of things until I learned about Sandy. Naturally, I went into a depression. Oh, I covered it; I had no choice. I couldn't let Sandy see me that way. I needed to be strong for her, but the depression was there. I knew it wouldn't be long before I'd need to get away for awhile.

Tracy's graduation day came. She received awards for A-B honor roll, 4-H and FHA; she was also homecoming queen that year. Tim sang, "That's What Friends Are For" at her graduation. The song was beautiful. Everyone was in tears. Tracey was beautiful, beaming as her brother sang. Tracy was working part time. She said she wanted to work full time and not go to college yet. She and Tonya (her best friend) wanted to get a place to live together. Her boyfriend gave her an engagement ring for graduation. I was happy for her but wished she would wait and enjoy herself before getting married.

Sandy was still out of it. The world was wrong and she was right about everything. We would get into it all the

Tracey, Homecoming Queen

Tracey's senior picture

Christmas 1986

time. Carmen, a friend from our church, came over a lot. She had always been good friends with the kids, so she spent time with Sandy. We all wanted to help her. One night Carmen came over and she, Sandy, Tracey and I rented some movies. We heard a commotion outside in the yard. As we got up to see what was going on, we saw our car being driven out of the yard. Tracey said she saw who was driving the car. It was him. He was stealing my car! I called the police to report my car being stolen. They told me that although the car was in my name, since he and I were still legally married they couldn't do anything.

He had stolen my car and gone to Boca Raton, Florida, to work with his brother in construction there. That was the only transportation we had. And living as we did in the boondocks, we had to have transportation. I called Mary and told her what had happened. She told me that I couldn't let him get away with stealing my car and that I should go get it. I took what savings I had left and bought an airline ticket for Boca Raton. He was not going to get away with this! I was tired of losing everything I worked for to men. Never again was I going to have to be the one to start over from scratch. I'd been the victim too often.

I called Mary back with the flight information, and she said that she and Mike would meet me in Boca Raton for security in case I had any trouble with him. They met me at the airport, and from there we went straight to the hotel where he was staying. We located the car in the parking lot and moved it several miles away. Then we went back. It was about 3 a.m. by this time, and we went to his room and knocked on the door. We had to knock several times before he came to the door and asked, "What is it?"

Mike answered, "Room service, sir. There appears to be a problem with your car."

Sandy, 9th grade

Tim with some friends: Sandy and
Carmen Gonzales are at far right

With that he opened the door, saying "What kind of problem?" Then he saw the three of us standing at the door.

I said, "The problem is yours. I'm taking my car back!" He stood there with his mouth open unable or afraid to say anything, particularly with another man there. I was able to see into the room and noticed a young, dark-skinned woman sitting up in the bed. I simply turned around and walked away. Mary, Mike and I went back to retrieve my car. Mary drove my car, and we went directly to her house in Jacksonville, a five-hour drive.

We were all pretty exhausted, but after we arrived we sat around and talked about what we did. Mike started laughing about the expression on his face. We all had a good laugh. I needed that!

Mike said, "Betty, you know we love you and you've been through so much. No more! You're staying with us."

"I can't," I replied. "The kids are—"

Before I could say anything more, Mary said, "The kids aren't kids anymore. Tim's in college, and Tracey has graduated and is getting married. You have to do this for you and Sandy. There is nothing keeping you there anymore."

The more she and Mike talked to me, the more sense it made. I told them to expect me back. With that response Mike said, "Betty, you have one week to get everything in order. If you're not on the road coming back here, I'm coming to get you, and you know I will!" I knew Mike and he meant it. I left the next day and drove back to Louisiana.

Chapter 18

When I got back to Louisiana, Tim was getting ready to move. He and his friends Ricky, Robby, Talmage and Warren had all rented a house together right by the campus. Tim was dating his first real girlfriend, Kim, who is a sweetheart. They came over and we all sat down, Tim, Sandy, Tracey and I told them about Mary and Mike's suggestion. They were all for it.

Tracey said, "Mom, I'm looking for a place. Tonya and I are going to get a trailer and rent it and be roommates."

I suggested that Tracey come with us. She said no. She wanted to get married and she had a job. I told her to come just for awhile, to put off getting married. "You've never been anywhere, Tracey. You're only 18. If you two are meant to be together, you will be." Well, she had her mind made up, and of course, moms don't know anything.

We all decided that the move was what Sandy and I needed to do. Maybe a change was just what Sandy needed. The next day, I went to work and gave my notice. Shirly and I had a good cry, but she agreed. We called Cathy; she came up and we all had a going-away party right then. They promised to visit me.

Things happened pretty fast after that moment. We put the house on the market (although it took several years to sell), and within two weeks, Sandy and I were gone. We stayed at Mary's house in Florida for about three weeks, just until I could get on my feet. Mary had four boys—Mike, Jay, Chris and Todd. Mike and Sandy were about the same age. The boys took to Sandy like a sister, and they all fought like brothers and sister, too. But the boys looked after her. Mary's husband, Mike, adored Sandy. They had always wanted a girl, so they adopted Sandy as their girl. I enrolled Sandy in school with Mary's older boys. And Mary got me a job at the radio station where she was working. The opening was for a receptionist, which was great since my head wasn't ready for bookkeeping. The money wasn't great, so I took a job at night as a cocktail waitress for extra money.

I can still remember when I brought my uniform home. It could fit in a small lunch bag! Sandy had a fit. "My mother is not wearing that!" She was so funny. Well, if I have to say so myself, I didn't look half bad. I wore it with a dancer's leotard. I was feeling healthy and proud of myself again, a feeling I hadn't had in a long time.

We got an apartment that wasn't much, but we were on our own. Tracy called one day and told us she had decided to get married. "What's the rush?" I said.

"I don't know. We just decided to do it and no Mom, I'm not pregnant," she informed me.

"I didn't ask that, Tracey."

She said, "I know but everyone else is."

There wasn't much time to prepare for the wedding, but she did all the preparations herself except the flowers, which I did. I worked on them at night after work. Tracey wanted silk, so I made them up in Florida and brought them with me to Louisiana. It was held at her husband's parents house and was really nice. Sandy and I drove there and took the flowers. But we could only stay Friday night and Saturday

Tim and his first steady
girlfriend, Kim

Tracey's wedding

and then rush home on Sunday, because I didn't have any vacation time yet.

I loved my job. The first year was the hardest, being away from Tim and Tracey. We went to visit as often as we could. The first Christmas, I didn't have any money so I used freebies from the station for presents: tapes and T-shirts. We went to my mom's to be with Tim. Tracey and her new husband came over; it was nice, but it made me miss them more.

Sandy was not coming around. Things actually got worse. I knew the problems were real, and I knew they probably did have something to do with him, but I didn't know what to do. I'd get calls that she wasn't at school, and I'd catch her over at a friend's house drinking and smoking. Finally, I just exploded. I said, "Fine, do what you want, but this is how it is. My door will lock at eleven o'clock. You will not get in after that time. No school, no allowance! You're on your own. If you can't go to school, study and come home on time: no car; you're walking." Finally after about six months of fighting with her, she came and apologized, asking if I would go to the school counselor with her and see what we could do to help with her grades. She'd failed everything and was two grades behind. So we did. The counselor was great. She said she really liked Sandy and knew there was a problem. We told her everything, and she recommended a school for girls, P.A.C.E. She set up an appointment. Sandy worked hard and went through counseling and went back to being the great girl I knew she was. She worked hard and graduated, got a job in retail and worked for a while.

I had gotten a promotion at work within the bookkeeping department, which meant more money. Tracey called and said she wanted to come visit. We hadn't seen her in so long, and she never called much. I was elated and so was Sandy, so I sent her a plane ticket (soon as they had a special on airfare). I could tell the minute she got here something was wrong; she was having problems. Her marriage wasn't working out. I won't go into detail, but she ended up moving to Florida and getting a divorce. The same year Tim called. He was unhappy at school and wanted to move, so he also came to Florida. Naturally, I was happy that all my kids would be together again.

Tracey, Sandy and I got a three-bedroom apartment. We only had one car, a red Ford Pinto. All of the girls' friends called it "the red Porsche." I worked days and Tracey worked nights in order to have transportation. As soon as I got home from work, Tracey would leave for her job.

Tim moved to Florida and stayed with us until he found an apartment. He enrolled in the junior college in Jacksonville and got an apartment and a part-time job. He still didn't have his mind on college. When he got here, he was already more into his music than school. He knew he had me to help him with it.

Mary's husband, Mike, was still playing music part time, so he and Tim started hanging out together. Mike took him to meet his musician buddies. Tim was self-taught on the guitar, and Mike helped him learn more about it. Tim plays very well.

Tim was still shy, so when Mike would take him to sit in with bands, they would have to coax him up on stage. After he finally got up he was fine, but it was getting him there that was the chore. He and Mike often went out at night to play music. Mike really helped Tim with his self-confidence. But all the music at night was interfering with Mike's job so he had to stop going with him. There aren't

Mary and Mike Reeves

Mary and Mike (Burnout)

many clubs in Jacksonville, and Tim really had the bug. He had the talent and now the fire, so he put a small band together and went back to Louisiana to play music.

He talked about moving to Nashville while he was here in Jacksonville. I told him we would go visit and see what Nashville was like as soon as we could save up enough money. He went back to Monroe, went back to college part time and played music. Tim was getting more and more serious about music.

Tracey was working as a waitress and wanted to go to nursing school. I had already left the radio station and was working as an office manager for the minor league baseball team in Jacksonville, the Expos. It was the same place where Tug played ball when I met him, but then it was the Suns. One day, Tracey came by the office and asked me if I'd go with her somewhere. When I asked where, she said, "The Army recruiter's office." I laughed. Tracey's 5'4", 115 pounds and cute as a button and she wanted to join the Army. She was serious, so we went.

I will tell you one thing, with the videos the recruiters show you and their sales pitch, if you're patriotic at all, they don't have to give you a hard sell. This was Friday, and she was ready to sign then. I suggested she go home and sleep on it over the weekend. She agreed. I even rented *Private Benjamin* for her to watch. I said, "Tracey, be sure. It's not easy." But she was already sold. I took her to the beach to walk and think like I used to do. I said, "Listen to the ocean. It will clear your mind so you can think clearly."

Tracey joined the Army to go into the nursing field after signing up and swearing in to "Good Old Uncle Sam." She didn't enter the nursing program. She ended up in the Signal Corps in communications and electronics. They told her that the nursing program she had signed up for was all filled up and that this was an open field that worked a lot with computers and would prove to be very promising. They also promised that upon her re-enlistment, she could transfer to nursing. This seemed okay with Tracey, as she really had no way out and was already enlisted. So once again her nursing plans were put on hold. Tim was back in Louisiana now and Sandy and I were still in Jacksonville.

Sandy came home one evening with a new fellow named Matt. They had met a few weeks earlier at the beach. She was now 18 and working at K-Mart. Matt was in the Navy and three years older than her. He was all she talked about. They were always together after that. I was glad she was working and had a steady boyfriend. I had been worried that all the painful things she had gone through with "him" had hurt her and she would not want a relationship. But she was adjusting and continuing with her therapy. It was all straightening out, and I was getting my old Sandy back.

One day, a Saturday, I was cleaning my apartment. I had invited a few friends from work for dinner. I love plants and have always had a house full of them, so I decided to go get a few more ivies and something blooming for my table. I went to Jones and Hall Nursery, which had been owned by my first boyfriend Jimmy's parents for years before Jimmy and his brothers took over the business. Jimmy was talking to a friend of his, Joe Trimble. They were evidently telling jokes, because they were all laughing loudly. Jimmy saw me and gave me a hug, and so did his brother John. Irvine, an old friend of Jimmy's who had been part his entourage when we were in school, was also there. They were all still great friends. Jimmy introduced me to Joe. He seemed like a very nice guy. He had a gruff-sounding voice and was 6'1", 185 pounds and six years older than I. He reminded me of Nick Nolte, the actor.

Tracey before the Army

GI Tracey

Jimmy said "Joe's been divorced for over a year, Betty. Do you have any girlfriends you can fix him up with?"

I said, "Probably. I'll see what I can do." I got my plants and went home.

A few days later at the office, I got a phone call from Joe. We talked for a while and soon we got to where we talked about every other day. We talked about everything. He had bookkeeping problems and I was a bookkeeper so that prompted a lot of conversations, and we also talked about our respective girlfriends and boyfriends. I fixed Joe up a couple of times, but they never clicked. Joe started calling me all the time, even when he couldn't sleep or had been out with his buddies. He would call me at midnight and we would talk. My girls had spoken to him on the phone a few times, although they'd not yet met him. They would say "Mom, you should date him. He sounds like a lot of fun."

I'd say, "No, we're just friends." And we remained good friends. In fact, he's still my best friend. I think that's why we get along so great.

About a year later, I had fixed Joe up with one of my friends from work. I had a date and we all went out. I guess Joe and I spent most of the time talking to each other because my friend excused herself to go to the rest room and motioned for me to join her.

"How come you and Joe don't date each other?" she said.

I replied, "We're just good friends and we're not interested in each other. We're too different."

She said, "Girl, you're blind. He's evidently already hooked on you and you're interested. You just haven't realized it yet." I couldn't say anything, I just looked at her.

We went back to the table and I guess I got too quiet thinking about what she had said.

Joe kept saying, "What's wrong with you, your cat die or what?"

"Joe, I don't have a cat." But, that's Joe.

Matt and Sandy became inseparable. One night they came in and announced they wanted to get married. I said, "That's great, but why don't you wait a while?" Matt seemed like a very nice young man. He was from a small town in Illinois. They hadn't known each other very long so they decided to wait. Well, three weeks later, they wanted to set a date. This was August so they picked September 23rd. (I'm so glad they listened to me and waited . . .) Well, that's the way things go. We all get in a hurry. So we started planning a wedding.

Sandy wanted to get married in Louisiana. That's where her dad was and my parents and most of her best friends. We planned a small wedding at my mom's church. It was small but nice. Sandy had chose a mauve pink for the color scheme, since pink was always her favorite color. As with Tracey's wedding, I did the flowers, white roses and orchids. We decorated the church with ivy, ferns, baby's breath and white ribbon. It was beautiful. Tracey couldn't make it to the wedding because of an Army commitment. Tim sang at the wedding. Sandy's father, Horace, gave her away. Just before the ceremony, Tim handed Matt the keys to his truck and said, "Okay, last chance to escape," But, he didn't. I think he was more nervous than anyone there. Sandy looked beautiful.

Joe called me several times while I was in Louisiana. He said he'd meet me in Tallahassee for dinner on my way back. He was going to be there for business. It was nine hours from my Mom's house to Tallahassee and another three on into Jacksonville. We met about 7 p.m. at his hotel and went to dinner. We had a wonderful time. I told him all

Horace and Sandy at her wedding

Tim

Tim singing at Sandy's wedding

about the wedding and told him the flowers his sister had sent were beautiful. I tried to get his sister's address to send money for the flowers, but he wouldn't let me. He said they were a wedding gift from him. It got late, and he suggested I get a room and go home in the morning. He was a real gentlemen and got me my own room. But needless to say, we didn't use it and we've been together ever since. Now when I think back, I realize we were beginning to have feelings for each other before then. When I returned, Joe and I began dating regularly. Since we had known each other for so long and were good friends, it wasn't long before we decided we wanted to be together. So a few months after Sandy got married, I moved in with Joe. Sandy and Matt were staying with me at the time, so I gave them my apartment all to themselves.

I think the hardest thing for me when Joe came into my life, was getting used to having someone help me. I was so used to doing things on my own and taking care of everyone else. Now I've got someone who wants to share the responsibilities. The first thing Joe wanted me to do was quit work, enjoy myself, do things for me for a change and not worry about everyone else. I did and it was a big adjustment. Now I help him in his business; we manufacture greenhouses. Since I love flowers and plants, I've been able to incorporate what I love into helping him. I can't be still; I have to be busy. I've been through a lot . . . but I've learned a lot. I catch myself being hard at times; when I watch a television program and it shows domestic abuse, I say why is that women being so stupid? Get away from him! When someone isn't getting her child support or is having problems with her children, I have to stop and think, "Been there. Done that." Friends come to me and my children's friends come to me and ask me questions.

Betty and Joe

Joe and Jimmy

I believe a man should take care of his child, no matter what the circumstances, but I do believe a woman should do her share. Don't take advantage of the system; be fair. He has to have a life also. He doesn't owe you, but he does owe his child.

As for abuse, well my philosophy on that is, the first time he hits you, it's his fault. After that, it's yours. . . . You're still there. Get out and take control.

Child abuse is sick, but it happens. Communicate with your children. When they have a drastic change in personality, something is wrong. Talk to them and find out what it is. We've all got to take back our lives and our children's lives.

Drugs, alcohol, and abuse: communication I think, is the key. I plan to visit abuse shelters and talk to women and children and go to schools and talk about peer pressure. If I can help change one life, it will be worth it.

The hardest thing for a woman to understand is you don't need another person in your life. When you can grasp that, then you will find the person you want in your life. I love Joe and we are good for each other. We know we don't need each other, but we do want each other and are very happy. I'm happy! Sometimes I feel down because I don't have anyone to take care of. Joe's as independent as I am, which is great. But I guess it's that empty nest syndrome people talk about. The kids have their lives, so I've got to let go and let them live. But it's hard. I'm just glad we all had the closeness we had, and I don't think that will change, even though we don't see each other as often as we used to. Tim's the one who's out of touch the most with all his traveling. I miss him a lot sometimes. I still manage to talk to him pretty often and my girls at least every other day. Joe's a wonderful man. We've been together over six years.

Chapter 19

Tim called me from Louisiana one weekend and said, "Mom, I need to talk to you. Just listen, Mom. Don't say anything until I'm finished. You know I'm not really doing well in school. I'm just not interested." (He was right. He was majoring in fraternity.) "You know how I feel about music. It's what I really want to do. I want to quit college, move to Nashville and pursue a singing career. If I don't have anything in two years, I'll go back to school and this time, I'll really study. I promise." I didn't say anything right away. Tim said, "Mom, are you there?"

"Yes, Tim." I thought for just a moment and said, "Well, you might as well. You're wasting time and money. If you don't do this, you'll always wonder 'What if?' So, give it a try while you've still got some of the money Tug set up for you and before you really get tied down in life. I say, go for it honey. Follow your dreams."

I don't think he believed me. "Really, Mom? Do you mean it?" he said.

Tim sold all his stuff and headed for Nashville. When he arrived in Nashville, he got an apartment and a roommate. He worked odd jobs and the usual "free" singing jobs in clubs around town like all star wannabes do. He made a lot of new friends.

One of his new friends was Danny Middleton. Danny was a single parent raising his son, Daniel, by himself. He

Tim, pre-Nashville

worked with his dad in a shopping cart repair business re-
pairing carts for major grocery store chains. Tim would go
on the road helping Danny when he needed money. Tim
says to this day he always checks the wheels on shopping
carts when he's in the stores. (Danny now works for Tim as
his farm manager. He takes care of everything for Tim since
he's on the road so much.) Another friend Tim made when
he first moved is Jimmy Frizell, a nephew of the late Lefty
Frizell. And of course, all new singers in Nashville have
been by Flash's Hound Dog Hot Dog Stand. Flash is known
for always feeding the out-of-work musicians around town.

About eight months after Joe and I moved into together,
my dad passed away. He had been in a nursing home for
several years, in bad health. So I needed to go to where he
had lived in Texas. I called the kids. Tim had been in the
studio working on his demos and was just finishing up. He
had an appointment with a record label, but he was going to
fly out to Texas for the funeral. He had to be back the next
day for his appointment. So Tim flew in from Nashville and
Joe drove me.

We all met at my brother Johnny's home in Texarkana.
Tim had to fly back out that evening. He had brought the
demo tape with him. Listening to it helped us all with the
solemn occasion. I knew my dad would have been proud of
him. As we listened to the tape, we all thought it was terrific. My mom kept wanting me to copy it. I finally got a tape
from my brother. I put it in his stereo, and not being fa-
miliar with his tape player, after I started it, I realized I had
put it in the wrong side, so I erased the first line. I was
already emotional because of my dad's funeral, so now I
was even more upset. I kept apologizing to Tim.

He said, "It's okay, Mom. It was an accident. I'll go first

thing in the morning and get another copy before my meeting."

I was so upset. I knew inside he was really wanting to choke me.

Tim made it back, got a new copy of his demo and made his meeting on time. His meeting was with Curb Records, and they signed him. I was ecstatic when he called to let us know. So one of the saddest times of my life was one of the happiest also. My dad would have been so proud. I always think of him in context with Tim's recording contract. My dad played the violin, so I know he'd be proud of Tim's career. (He's probably in heaven playing Tim's songs on a violin for all the angels.)

Tim and his band were doing gigs, but little changed at first. Tim was working on picking songs for his first album. I had managed to help them book a few dates. One evening Tim called me from Texas. He said, "You know, Mom, if I had T-shirts and pictures to sell, I could make some extra money to help with expenses." We talked a little longer and after we hung up I started thinking. I told Joe what Tim had said about T-shirts. We talked about it and the next day we went to see a couple of people who made T-shirts. Joe had shirts made and pictures printed up and we mailed them out to Tim. Joe and I were getting along great. We grew closer everyday. I finally was finding out what real love was all about. The T-shirts and pictures sold pretty well. Every now and then, one of those old shirts will show up at a concert.

Tim started a fan club, and Kelly Wright became its president. She's the one who started calling me "McMom." Now, everyone calls me that—not Betty Trimble, just McMom.

Tim with fan club president Kelly Wright at Fan Club Party

The Dancehall Doctors
John Marcus, Darren Smith, Dean Brown, Bob Minner, Denny Hemingson,
Billy Mason, and Jeff McMahon—*Photo by Peter Orth*

The Army sent Tracey to Germany and I planned to go over for a visit. Then one day, she called and said she had orders for Saudi Arabia. She was so upset, and I don't have to tell you, so was I. I stayed calm for her, and then Joe came home and I went to pieces. He's the only person I can come unglued with. I had a good cry and then tried to deal with the facts. Joe took me on a vacation to Atlantic City while Tracey was in Saudi to help get my mind off the Gulf War and most of all, my little girl being in Desert Storm. When it was all over, she elected to take the early out they offered all the enlisted personnel and came home to Florida.

Tracy liked the Army, but I think being in Desert Storm scared her. She'd say, "Man, I can't believe how they treat women there. You get on a bus and it's partitioned off and all the women are to sit in the back. We'd get on the bus and the guys would tell us girls to go to the back. I'd sit right behind the driver! I'd tell them if I'm over here, supposed to be putting my life on the line, I'm sitting where I want to. It was the same in restaurants and stores. Women had to go in the back door." Tracey said she marched right in the front door and no matter what anyone said, she'd just keep walking. The men would tell her to go to the back and she'd say, "Not me Mister."

I was glad she was home. She moved in with Joe and me, got a job and started going to school to be a nurse.

Sandy's husband was stationed at Mayport, and Sandy was working in Joe's office.

Joe and I had been together over three years when one night we decided to get married. We made no big plans; we just decided to go elope to a Justice of the Peace. The night before, Joe called Tim in Nashville and asked if it was all right for him to marry me.

Tim said, "Yeah, Joe, I think it's great. What took you so long? Do you think you can put up with her?" He laughed. "Really, I think it's great. My mom loves you and she needs someone who will love her and be good to her for a change, and I know you will." Joe handed me the phone. Naturally, I was crying. Tim said, "Mom, it's great. I'm so happy. When's the wedding?" I told him we were just going to elope. We said good-bye and hung up. Then we called Mary and Jimmy, and the next day, we did it. Mary was my matron of honor and Jimmy was Joe's best man. We all went for a late lunch afterwards. Two days later we went on a honeymoon in Tampa, where we attended a trade show. From there, I called the girls, Joe called his boys and we both called our moms.

Joe's been great. He's good to my kids and he's getting used to being a grandpa to my three-year-old grandchild. Joe's not comfortable with small kids, but he's learning. He's got two boys, Joe Jr., who's 25 and Chris, who's 21. He was a salesman, always on the road, when they were little, but he's getting better at this stuff. I've never been happier. I feel loved and cared for and comfortable. If you're not comfortable with your partner, something's wrong. I thank God everyday for Joe. He's a gruff old bear on the outside and a big ole Teddy bear on the inside, and we're as happy as two peas in a pod.

So now I'm married to a guy who was introduced to me

WILLIAM "CRAIG" MILLER
1846 HIGHWAY 211 N.W.
HOSCHTON, GA 30548-3519

TP'67

ORANGE PARK
JUL-8'97
FL

U.S. POSTAGE
0070
METER 469337

TERRY PARKER CLASS of 1967 — 30 YEAR REUNION
Friday and Saturday, July 11 & 12, 1997
Sea Turtle Inn, Atlantic Beach, Florida

We have received your registration for your reunion, and your reservation is confirmed as follows:

```
                                      TP '67

WILLIAM "CRAIG" MILLER
# ATTENDING FRIDAY:           2
# ATTENDING SATURDAY:         2
# CLASS PHOTOS ORDERED:       0
DEPOSIT PAID:           $150.00
BALANCE DUE:              $0.00
```

If there is a balance due, please return this card and your payment to:
Class Reunion, PO Box 897, Orange Park, FL 32067-0897
For information and questions, call: (904) 269-5471

by my first boyfriend from when I was 16 years old, my first love. Now twenty-something years later, I'm marrying his best friend and he's best man at our wedding. How's that for coming almost full circle? It's wonderful that we're all great friends. I'm happier than I've ever been. Life with Joe is never dull . . . but Joe's a whole other book. He's a character in himself. And I have to say, I love this man with all my heart and soul.

Sandy and her husband, Matt, blessed me with the bundle of joy on December 31, 1991. A New Year's Eve baby. He's my joy now. A grandchild is a special kind of love all its own. I'm enjoying my grandchild, Matthew. He's three now and comes to visit at least once a month for a couple of days. My life is never boring. I'm always busy.

Tim's new album is out, and he's working hard. He and the band are doing more and more traveling. Now they have a bus instead of Tim's yan and a truck. Tim hired a road manager, Mark Hurt, about the same time the first album, Tim McGraw was released. They are still together on the road. Mark, as well as all the other guys who work with Tim, have become like family. My family grows everyday. They are all terrific people. Tim's manager, Tony Harley, is a real sweetheart. These people all take good care of my son. I thank all of them. I couldn't ask for nicer people in my son's corner than Eric and Ree, his business manger and accountant. Tim also has two of his college roommates working with him, Robbie Cucullu and Ricky Hooter. These boys have been like brothers since Tim's first year of college.

When the album Tim McGraw came out, it was a good album and two songs went Top 40. It kept them on the road, but air play was not terrific. I would call the stations here and bug them to death. I know they got tired of hearing

Matt, Sandy and Matthew

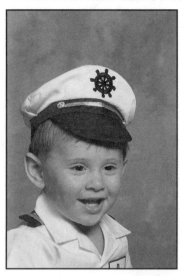

Matthew

MeMaw, PePaw and Matthew

Betty and Tim at Fan Fair '93

Tim and Tug in '93

from me. I've worked in radio off and on, so I had a few friends like Robbie Rose and John Richards, at one of the stations here. I would call and they would say, "Betty, you know we only play Top 30." They did play "Welcome to the Club" some. I got Tim a job playing at a yearly festival called the "Ham Jam," and their station was a sponsor. They played the song to promote the event. Also, I was able to get him a job opening for Gene Watson at the fair in Jacksonville that same year.

We made a big deal out of it, since it was his first job opening and it was at the Coliseum, the same building I had danced in. My Aunt Dink and cousins Sammy Pearl and Angie flew in. Tug's wife, Phyllis, and Tim's half-brother, Mark, and half-sister, Carrie, were there also. We had a big party for Tim and the band.

The next single was "Memory Lane." It didn't do as well as "Welcome To The Club," but I still like that song. I was still calling both stations here requesting Tim's songs. After "Indian Outlaw" came out and it went Top 30, I called Robbie and John at WROO. As soon as they answered the phone that morning, I just said, "Na, Na, Na, Na. Tim McGraw is Top 30!" They laughed. We are great friends, and now they call me. Thanks guys! (And you too, Dee.) Now, I don't have to call WROO and WQIK in Jacksonville; both play Tim's music all the time now.

In March 1994, Tim's second album, Not A Moment Too Soon, was released. The first single off the album was "Indian Outlaw." It sky-rocketed, and Tim had a hit on his hands. The album debuted at number one and stayed there for 26 weeks. Although "Indian Outlaw" only went to number eight in the singles charts, it launched a new country music singer. With "Indian Outlaw" came the controversy. A few Native Americans took offense at some of the

Photo taken of Tim on stage by Tracey

words in the song. This upset Tim. He didn't write the song, but the song was meant in fun, not to be taken seriously. Tim finally reconciled himself to the fact some people were not going to like it. He decided if it caused people to listen to the problems of all Native Americans, he was glad.

The second single released off the album was "Don't Take the Girl." This was Tim's first number one single. This song helped prove Tim McGraw does have what it takes to stick around. The title cut, "Not a Moment Too Soon," is my favorite. I love the video, and I tell Sherman Halsey (the producer/director) it's my very favorite.

I think that song will be special to me for a long time. The words, taken spiritually, fit my life. God's always been there for me, or maybe I should say with me, and helps me "Not a Moment Too Soon." I can remember one time having my electricity cut off because I couldn't pay the bill. That same evening I received a check from someone for doing the flowers for her daughter's wedding; it paid my electric bill.

Tim's career took off pretty fast. By the time the album had been out four months, it was triple platinum and had two gold singles, something no one else had achieved in quite a while. Tim's achieved a lot over the last year. More than he and I ever dreamed. It's great! Now I'm the proud mother of a country music star. He sends me on trips, shopping and to see his concerts. He bought his two sisters each a car. You can't imagine the thrill of hearing him on the radio. It's just great when your kids succeed in something they really wanted. Naturally with success comes award shows, and I guess that's a mom's high, when other people see what you've always known.

Tim was nominated for a Jukebox Award for Most Played New Artist in 1994. He couldn't attend, so he sent

Sherman Halsey (Tim's video producer) and Tim

Tim and Byron Gallimore (Tim's Producer)

me to accept for him. His award was presented to me by
Rita Coolidge, who is one of my favorite singers. I was so
nervous. I don't remember what I said, but I was indeed the
proud mom. The award is hanging on my wall. Next came
the CMA (Country Music Association) Awards. Tim was
nominated for two awards: Song of the Year and Single of
the Year. Although he didn't win, I was in the audience to
see my son"s first performance on national television. You
just can't imagine how it feels seeing him singing on the
stage. I had watched these shows for years; now my baby
was up there.

In May were the AMA's (American Music Awards), a
Dick Clark award show. This award show covers all music.
Tim won New Male Vocalist. When Clint Black said, "The
winner is . . .," I was sitting between Tim's girlfriend and
his manager. I had my fingers crossed and my head down.
Clint Black said, "Tim McGraw," and I started crying. I
looked over at Tim, and he reached over and gave me a big
hug and a kiss. I stood up and applauded. Everyone around
me was congratulating me. He got up there and said, "This
is for my mom for being a dreamer and instilling that in
me." It was wonderful.

Sitting there as Tim accepted his award, I thought about
that night, more that 27 years ago, when I first realized I
was pregnant with him. I had an audition letter sitting on the
table for Dick Clark's "Where The Action Is," which I
wouldn't be making. And now, I was sitting at a Dick Clark
award show watching my son accept an award as well as
perform on an award show. My life truly has many circles.

The awards didn't stop there. Next came the ACM's
(Academy of Country Music) in Los Angeles. Tim flew
Tracey, Sandy and me out there. "E" News was there to
film a special on Tim. They followed the girls and me as we

l to r: Manager Tony Harley, Mike Curb, Tim,
Byron Gallimore, and James Stroud

Sandy, Tim, Betty, and Tracey at the ACMs

Tim and Road manager, Mark Hurt

Betty and her parents at Fan Fair

Carman and Tim at Fan Fair

Betty and Joe at the CMAs

Tim's grandfather and grandmother at the CMAs

got ready. Tim was nominated for four awards: New Artist, Song of the Year, Single of the Year, and Album of the Year. "E" News asked my predictions, and I said, "Naturally, I'm hoping for a clean sweep, but I think he will get New Artist and Album of the Year."

I had picked right. He won big . . . New Artist and Album of the Year. I was so elated, I was jumping up and down. My girls said, "Mom, please sit down." He accepted the award and said, "Hey . . . Mom, Tracey and Sandy, how do you like LA?" It was the best feeling anyone could have. I was so glad that all four of us were there together, like it's always been, bad times and good times . . . together!

I'm so proud of all three of my kids:
Sandy the Mom,
Tracey the Nurse
and Tim the Artist.
No Mother could be more PROUD!
The End

Epilogue

It has been very hard for me to write this book. I never really had to talk about what happened to me and probably never would except my son Tim did grow up to be somebody. Because of all the coverage with the press and everyone wanting to know about him . . . the story just had to come out.

In the '60s, if you were an unwed mother you were looked down on. You weren't a nice girl. Well my pride kept me going and kept me from contacting Tug. I'm not ashamed, I'm proud. I'm proud of me and I hope my children are, also. I know I was a good mother, and now I'm their good friend.

I lost a lot in 1966: I gave up high school, graduation, senior prom, college, and my youth. I was forced to grow up and become a mother. I thank God everyday for my wonderful baby son, but it wasn't easy. That's why I say, "Girls, be careful." A child is great and I wouldn't trade any of mine for anything in this world, but children deserve for their mom to be all she can be. If I hadn't been a strong person it could have turned out different."

So don't let anyone talk you into sex before you're ready. Give yourself time to grow and enjoy your youth. Have fun, do all you want to do, and be the best person you can be and you'll make a great parent.

My three kids are my life. We went through a lot, but we had enough love to get us through.

Hope you enjoyed my book.

God Bless.

"McMOM"

Mary Reeves and Betty "McMom" Trimble

Betty "McMom" and Diana Henderson

The city of Start named a street after Tim

Tim

Tim with his dog Whitley

Mark Lindsey (Paul Revere and the Raiders) and Tim at Fan Fair '94

Tim as "Casey at the Bat"

Credits

Estelle Barefield
Tommy Barnes
Sammie Pearl Belguard
Charlotte Bergeron
Bradford's Furniture
Clara Forbes Bragg
Barney Bryant
Curtis Bryant
Coach and Mrs. Butler
Lance Butler
Irvin Byrd
Curb Records
Angie Coronado
Jene Coronado
Robbie Cuculla
John Dagostino
John Dagostino Jr.
Eric Dahlhauser
Dee Davenport
Sandy DeLettre
Delhi Clinic
Billie DiGiovanni
Ree Ditmore
Catherine Doctors
Herb Doctors
Dance Hall Doctors
Clara Ann Driggers
Sandy Everett
Matt Everett
Matthew Everett
Gregg Franklin
Carmen Gonzalas
Betty Guynes
Jimmy Hall
Tony Harley
Dee & Barbara Harper
Ricky Hooter
Mark Hurt
Jax Suns/Expos

Dr. Lester Johnson
Judy Jordan
Johnny Kimbrough
Pearl Kimbrough
Shirly & Jessie Lee
Tom & Kathy McCartney
Margret McCartney
Carrie & Mark McGraw
Phylis McGraw
Tim McGraw
Tug McGraw
Marilyn Metzer
Tracey Miller
Terry Parker High School
Wayne Perry
Regina Raney
Mary Reeves
Mike, Jay, Chris &
    Todd R. Reeves
Bubba Redding
John Richard
Robbie Rose
Cathy "Bubbles" Stringer
    Sanders
Cathy Smith
Claude & Margret
    Templeton
Ken Templeton
Chris & Joe Trimble
Joe Trimble
Hank & Tickle Wallace
Buddy Welch
Margret Welch
Bobby Wilson
Mark Wilson
Kelly Wright
WQIK
WROO

ORDER FORM

Use this form to order additional copies of
Tim McGraw
A Mother's Story
or to receive a free Tim McGraw catalog.

Name: _____

Address: _____

City: _____ St:___ Zip: _____

Daytime phone: (_____)_____

    If gift, message that you would like enclosed: _____

_____

_____

_____

    If gift, ship to:

    Name _____

    Address: _____

    City: _____ St:___ Zip: _____

Method of Payment: *(Make payable to **mcgrawfunaddicts**)*

    ❏ Check ❏ Money Order ❏ VISA ❏ MasterCard

Card# _____ Exp. _____

Signature: _____
    Required for credit card purchases

Quantity: ___ x $21.95 =	$_____
Shipping & Handling Quantity: ___ x $4.00 =	$_____
Sub Total:	$_____
TN residents add 8.25% sales tax	$_____
Total:	$_____

Please return form and payment to: **mcgrawfunaddicts™**
    p.o. box 128138
    nashville, tn 37212

FOR FASTER SERVICE CALL 1–800–776–3650

Thank You!
Your order will be shipped within 1-3 weeks from receipt